PLANNING AND CITIES

GEORGE R. COLLINS, Columbia University
General Editor

NEW TOWNS:
ANTIQUITY TO THE PRESENT

ERVIN Y. GALANTAY

GEORGE BRAZILLER, NEW YORK

To the Memory of my brother Tibor
killed in October 1956, Budapest

QUI ANTE DIEM PERIIT · SED MILES · SED PRO PATRIA

For information address the publisher:
George Braziller, Inc. One Park Avenue, New York, N.Y. 10016
Library of Congress Catalog Card Number: 74–81216
International Standard Book Number: 0–8076–0766–5, cloth
0–8076–0767–3, paper

Printed in the U.S.A.
First printing

GENERAL EDITOR'S PREFACE

As today we build new towns all over the Earth and contemplate the planning of them on other heavenly bodies, it behooves us to consider the meaning of the "new town" in other than its conventional twentieth-century usage.

In this series of books on cities and planning we have tried to include not only volumes dealing with specific historical periods, geographical regions, and important individuals, but also studies of influential concepts surveyed in their inception and development. Our volume on the influence of fortification theory and practice is an example of this, and we hope to publish analyses of Ideal Cities and other conceptual types.

Certainly one of the liveliest subjects—literally—in the history of planning and cities is the new town, and I therefore asked one of the liveliest minds that I know in the field—Ervin Y. Galantay—to take on the subject. He has done so with a perspective that ranges over time and space even more widely than I had hoped. And he speaks with authority: not only has his career involved the teaching of the subject and historical research into abstruse but important nooks and crannies—e.g., the Catalan Eiximenis—but in addition he has worked on teams that have planned influential contemporary new towns.

Our aim in these books is to give the newcomer a general view of the subject and an insight into its actualities and problems, backed up with plentiful illustrative material. Our author has, I think, admirably fulfilled our intentions. While the scope chosen inevitably leads to some shortcuts and generalizations, he has managed to direct rather than deaden the reader by using his extensive knowledge of data not in a simple factual and descriptive way, but rather to indicate the problems and controversies that each supposed solution has triggered. By his ingenious use of typologies to organize his chapters and then their contents, he has cut through what would otherwise be simply a recitation of facts. And, lastly, he has aided us, by his comprehensiveness and personal interests, to get ourselves out of the conventional byways of modern Western culture and to deal with several of today's "worlds" and societies. We started our volumes some years ago with the "primitive" and the pre-Columbian peoples; texts on other non-Western cultures such as China and Japan, Southeast Asia, and the Moslem peoples will be forthcoming.

July, 1974   G.R.C.

CONTENTS

PREFACE

The literature of new towns is abundant but consists of books written by planners for planners or deals with selected periods of new town building from the viewpoint of the economist or the architectural historian.

In this volume I have attempted to achieve a synthesis by tracing the origins of new town concepts and by applying the performance criteria of modern planning to the analysis of new town building in history. This approach requires reference to certain quantitative indices such as the target population, growth rate, area, and density.[2]

To provide a simple structure for the volume, I have divided the vast material typologically in four main chapters: new capitals, colonial towns, planned industrial towns, and decongestion. Each chapter is an independent essay and consists of definitions, a historical survey, and case studies—leading to a bibliography which should permit those interested to follow up different aspects of new town building barely mentioned here, such as ideal cities and utopian communities.

In line with the objectives stated by the general editor I have emphasized formal concepts, without neglecting the economic and social determinants of new town building. Although I am an urban designer rather than a historian I strived to follow Sigfried Giedion's advice to "uncover for our own age vital interrelations with the past . . . by searching out aspects which are significant concerns of our own period and thus offer insights into the moving process of life." [1]

My thanks go to numerous colleagues and friends who have helped in my research. My special gratitude to Prof. Lloyd Rodwin of MIT, Prof. J. Dyckman of Berkeley, and Mr. M. Hoppenfeld from Columbia, Md. for stimulating discussions on the occasion of the 1972 Salzburg Seminars; to Prof. A. Ling, Nottingham; Prof. W. Custer and P. Hofer at the ETH (Swiss Federal Institute of Technology), Zürich for helpful comment and—last but not least—to George Collins for the encouragement to begin—and to complete—this volume.

E.G.
Swiss Federal Institute of Technology,
Lausanne.

1 INTRODUCTION

Definitions New towns are planned communities consciously created in response to clearly stated objectives. Town creation as an *act of will* [1] presupposes the existence of an authority or organization sufficiently effective to secure the site, marshal resources for its development, and exercise continued control until the town reaches viable size.

New towns have an identifiable date of birth which may be the day of the designation of their site or the day of a formal act of foundation bestowing legal or ritual existence to the new community. The "idea" of the town is formalized in a plan prepared before the site is altered by the arrival of the first new residents. Once started, new towns are rapidly built to achieve "critical mass" within a crucial initial time span. This process is in sharp contrast to the genesis and evolution of the towns of an "organic" or agglomerate type which emerge from preurban nuclei, and grow by a slow and sometimes disjointed process of uncoordinated actions. The plan of a new town is based on estimates of the growth potential of the new community which permits the fixing of a "target" population. Such a "target" is necessary to be able to make adequate provision for the physical and social needs of the future. Obviously such needs depend not only on numbers but also on the culture and the relative economic development of the society which is building the new town.

Recently the concept of a fixed finite size is being replaced by a more flexible framework providing for successive stages of development. The vision of a preconceived town form represented by a "Master Plan" is rejected in favor of "strategic plans" providing for "alternative futures"—alternative modes of spatial development with different timetables and investment scenarios.

Colonial towns, new capitals, and planned industrial towns were often built on virgin land. By contrast, new towns located within metropolitan areas are not only contiguous to existing development but their site often includes sizable established settlements. No wonder that the term "new town" has become ambiguous, since it is often misleadingly employed to advertise suburban tract-development.

To limit our discussion we propose to exclude the so-called "new towns-in-town," which are large-scale urban renewal projects within the boundaries of a central city. On the other hand we shall include "extended towns" and "satellites"—built to decongest the central cities or to restructure the haphazard land-use tissue of a conurbation. Although "extended towns" and "satellites" retain varying degrees of dependence on a central city, they are planned to become relatively balanced communities with distinct identity. In expanded towns such as the villes nouvelles of the Paris region the newcomers will outnumber the autochthonous residents tenfold, and the proposed new town structure will change the present pattern of land use beyond recognition.

Economic base

An important element for the comparison of new towns is their employment base. A new town is *balanced* if it has a complete age-sex mix and its job provision corresponds to the number of potential job-seekers. This theoretical balance does not exclude the possibility of some exchange of "in-and-out commuting"—such as occurs also in established towns. A balanced town is not necessarily *self-contained* which would imply a considerable degree of self-sufficiency expressed in the composition of the employment. Obviously the town's residents cannot live by "taking in each other's laundry." Ideally a self-contained town should have a fixed ratio of jobs in "basic" industries (working for export and bringing in money from the outside) to "nonbasic" employment (providing goods and services for consumption by the town's own residents). However it would be simplistic to view only manufacturing as a "basic" industry since various "export" services can also bring income to the town from the outside: as exemplified by capital cities, resort towns, or towns based on education or research.

Since the "basic-nonbasic" ratio is an index of urban interdependence it is obvious that a new town in an isolated location must be more self-contained then a town located within a metropolitan area where self-sufficiency occurs on a regional scale and therefore a large degree of specialization is possible.

New towns in history and in the evolution of societies

New towns have been created throughout history by different civilizations but not as a continuous activity: waves of new town building alternated with long periods of calm and lack of interest. In explanation of this phenomenon we may advance the hypothesis that the need for new towns arises at transitional phases in the evolution of a society. Each "new town wave" represents an effort to develop a new community structure that would correspond to the changed economic base. In this, new towns serve as prototypes for the subsequent restructuring and modernizing of the large cities.

According to Colin Clark and Jean Fourastié [2] the evolution of urban societies is expressed by the changing composition of the active population by employment categories (Fig. 1):

— In a primary—or *preindustrial society*—the vast majority of the population is engaged in agriculture.

— In an *industrial society* 30% or more of the labor force is employed in the production of goods, with a decreasing percent-

1 The evolution of human
  societies in terms of the
  employment composition.

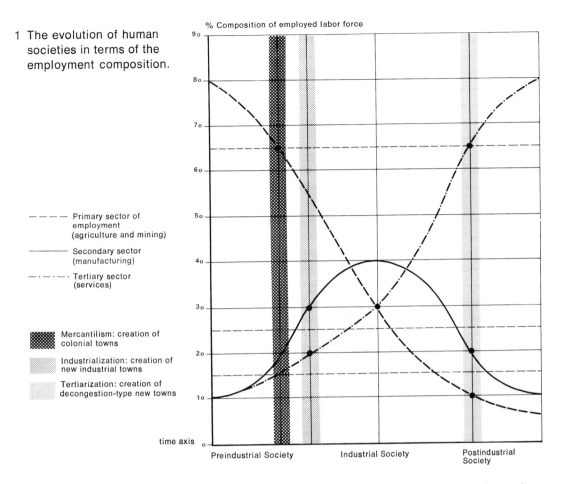

% Composition of employed labor force

— — — Primary sector of
employment
(agriculture and mining)

———— Secondary sector
(manufacturing)

— · — · — Tertiary sector
(services)

▓▓ Mercantilism: creation of
colonial towns

▒▒ Industrialization: creation of
new industrial towns

░░ Tertiarization: creation of
decongestion-type new towns

time axis

Preindustrial Society   Industrial Society   Postindustrial
                                               Society

age in agriculture and an increasing percentage in various
"services."

— Finally in a *postindustrial* or tertiary *society* the percentage of those employed in agriculture is stabilized below 10%;
there is a steady decrease in the manufacturing sector and an
ever-larger percentage of the population is employed in various
"tertiary" activities: administration, commerce, communications, education, and research.

In accordance with our theory the *colonial towns* of preindustrial societies were founded in response to an enlargement of the mercantile sector which provided the risk capital
for the colonizing venture. The creation of mining towns
and of administrative centers was simply instrumental to the
achievement of the main goal of expanding long distance
trade. Internal colonization by the creation of new *industrial
towns* is characteristic of the transition from preindustrial to
industrial society. Western countries completed this phase
during the nineteenth century and Eastern Europe with a
considerable time-lag between 1900–1950. Latin America, Africa, and Asia (including the Asiatic half of the Soviet Union)
are presently in various stages of this transition and are therefore vitally involved in the creation of industrial towns as instru-

ments of forced modernization. Similarly the problem of *decongestion* of large cities by the creation of satellites and expanded towns heralds the transition from industrial to a postindustrial society oriented toward leisure and consumption, with a predominance of white-collar jobs.

These insights at first suggested a simple chronological presentation of preindustrial, industrial, and postindustrial new towns. However to such an approach we preferred a *typological* division based on the primary function of the new towns. This is achieved in the chapters on industrial towns or on decongestion which correspond to the evolutionary phases of our key hypothesis. On the other hand we grouped together ancient and modern new capitals and towns resulting from external and internal colonization in order to emphasize their genetic ties and morphological similarities.

2 NEW CAPITALS

Definitions New capital cities are built for one of two reasons: the first and most obvious is the creation of a new state; the second, the need to transfer the government from an existing to a more advantageous location.

New states emerge by political change or territorial reorganization. Former colonies gaining independence may require a new capital as a symbol of national identity. Territorial change may also deprive a region of its traditional center, imposing on it the creation of a new capital as in the case of the Punjab State of India. There the loss of Lahore, which went to Pakistan after the partition, prompted the decision to build Chandigarh. If the new state is forged by the confederation of previously distinct political entities the location of a new capital on a virgin site may offer a compromise solution between competing regions and cities: Washington D.C. was founded to maintain an equilibrium between the northern and southern States of the Union; and Canberra was created to overcome the rivalry of Melbourne and Sidney. The transfer of the capital may be prompted by strategic reasons such as the desire to move away from a threatened frontier, or by the reverse goal of moving closer to the border in the vanguard of anticipated expansion (St. Petersburg [Leningrad], Islamabad, Changan).

Geopolitical considerations often dictate the transfer of the capital from the periphery to a more central position in the national territory. Such a move may also serve a national policy aimed at opening up undeveloped areas of the country by furthering demographic redistribution. The best example for this is the creation of Brasilia, built, in the words of President Kubitschek, to draw the population away from the Atlantic coast, where "Brazilians cling like crabs to the crowded shorelines." [1]

A government pursuing a modernization policy may find it expedient to move its capital from a city closely identified with the traditions and inertia of an *ancien régime.* If the capital is to serve as the vehicle of an outward-looking policy aimed at importing new skills, a different culture, or a new social order a more peripheral location for the capital might be desirable. Such was the case of Alexandria, capital of Ptolemaic Egypt, culturally and commercially oriented toward Greece, or St. Petersburg in Russia, created by Peter I as "a window to the West." In turn, Lenin moved the government back to Moscow to eliminate the stifling mementos of the Romanov dynasty, and similar considerations prompted Kemal Atatürk in 1923 to make his capital in Ankara instead of Istanbul as a sign of his break with the Ottoman Empire.

The location of the new capital may be a virgin site or else the capital can be juxtaposed on an existing city. Starting *ex nihilo* has the disadvantage of having to import not only material but also the labor force (Brasilia). By contrast, an existing settlement will provide the necessary manpower pool and basic services during the crucial construction phase. Eventually the new capital may completely eclipse and absorb the original town or form a twin city with it in a symbiotic division of functions, as proposed for Rawalpindi-Islamabad. The location of a new capital has tremendous impact on the regional and national economy. It invariably triggers the construction of new communication lines—canals, highways, railroads—along which strings of new settlements arise. In view of this, the location should be chosen on the basis of a careful analysis of alternatives. Nonetheless, political opportunism often prevails over considerations of economic geography.

As Major L'Enfant, the planner of Washington D.C., shrewdly observed, "the capital city's nourishments, unlike that of other cities would come out of its public buildings rather than out of its trade centers."[2]

By taxation, the government brings in money from outside of the region of the capital, and the concentration of power and wealth draws in further "unearned" income which can be spent for local services and representative buildings. Since capital cities consume more than their share of the national revenue they are often denounced as "parasitic"; it is then urged that their economic base be widened by bringing in manufacturing industry. This may be feasible in countries with large reservoirs of marginally employed manpower. By contrast, in developed countries the pay rate of government employees makes capital cities into a "high salary area" and hence a poor choice for industry to locate. In fact the basic "industry" of capital cities is the central-office function of the government exporting its services to the rest of the country. Government employment will tend to dominate unless nongovernment "export" services of national scope are developed. Such services as higher education, banking, research, tourism may offer an important counterpoint.

Historical survey

Near East The first planned towns in history may well have been the capitals of ambitious rulers. Different rulers of the same dynasty sometimes built new capitals for reasons of superstition, prestige, or strategy.

Akhetaten (El Armana) is the first example of a new capital built as an instrument of cultural reform (1475–1358 B.C.). The Pharaoh Akhenaten moved the capital from Thebes to escape the pressure of the orthodox priest cast. The hastily built large town shows as yet no evidence of an overall plan.[3]

It is in eighth-century Mesopotamia that we first encounter what appear to be preconceived geometric plans, Dur Sharrukin (Khorsabad), the capital of Sargon II, was a squarish trapezoid of 300 ha. In sixth-century Borsippa (Birs Nimrud) —of 405 ha—a clear functional differentiation between palace, temple district, and living quarters of the population is evident.[4]

Alexandria, one of the numerous provincial capitals founded by Alexander the Great, was planned around 331 B.C. by Deinocrates of Rhodes. The town apparently had a grid plan of the colonial type with wide streets (Plate 1) covering 1,300 ha., which implies that a large population was envisaged and in fact its inhabitants numbered at least 300,000 by 21 B.C.[5]

After Alexander, most of the Middle East followed the Hellenistic trend toward orthogonal layouts. An independent tradition prevailed, however, in Persia where new capitals were frequently laid out in a circular pattern. Ctesiphon built by the Parthians around 129 B.C. was an oval of 3,300 m. × 2,800 m. Darabjerd, founded somewhat later, is described as a near perfect circle of 1,187 m. diameter with two concentric ringwalls, and Isfahan also as "evenly round" with 3,000 m. diameter. According to Arab historians, Darabjerd served as a model for the great city of Gur (Firuzabad) built by Ardashir I, founder of the Sassanid dynasty, in 226 A.D. The plan of Gur was a circle, "as though drawn with a compass," with 2,240 m. diameter and four gates, built as a symbol of the sundial with a fire tower in its middle.[6]

Five hundred years later, under the Abbasid khalifs, the Muslim world came under Persian influence and the memory of Gur was revived with the creation of Baghdad under Khalif al-Mansur (Plate 2). Built from 762–766 A.D., in the record time of four years, the city was a perfect circle of 2,638 m. diameter enclosing an area of about 500 ha. In a symbol of "paradise on earth," the central area was reserved for a vast garden with a mosque, the palaces, and seven government departments or *Diwans*.[7] An annular area 300 m. wide built between the inner and outer walls accommodated 45 residential wards and may have housed 30,000 people, presumably court employees and the guard troops from Khurasan. By the time of Khalif Harun al-Rashid (786–809 A.D.), Baghdad had become the greatest city of Islam. The city grew in an agglomerate fashion around the circular core covering some 6,000 ha., accommodating 120,000–200,000 people. The planning history and dimensions of this town are well known, as they were described by numerous eye-witnesses.[8] Nevertheless, after only seventy years as a capital, Baghdad was abandond in favor of Samarra and by the time it again became a capital the structure of the circular city had disappeared. With this experiment, the planning of radioconcentric new capital cities disappears until the idea returns with Tommaso Campanella's *Civitas Solis* (1623) and the building of Grammichele (1693) and Karlsruhe (1715).[9]

Chinese Capitals By contrast, Far Eastern town planning, and particularly the planning of new capitals, has long been codified to reflect cosmological speculation. *Chou-Li*—the book of rules of the Chou dynasty (1122–256 B.C.)—formally prescribes layout and size of a new capital city. The plan of Chou-Wang-Cheng was a square with three gates on each side, nine streets running east to west and nine streets north to south. The Imperial Palace is in the middle, with the administration compound in front of the palace and the market place behind it. The ancestral temple is to the left, the Altar of the Soil to the right. The size of the inner town was to be 9 li or about 325 ha.[10]

Later Chinese capital cities like Lo-Yang modified the Chou ideal plan; the shape of the town becomes a rectangle with the palace moved from the center into a "head" position in the middle of the north wall.[11]

The Chinese model found its most nearly perfect formulation in Changan (Plate 3). Planned in 580 A.D., Changan served during three centuries as the capital of the brilliant T'ang dynasty.

An immense rectangle of 15×18 li (9,991 m. $\times$ 8,446 m.) covered 8,438 ha. or 84.38 km. square—the size of Manhattan. Apart from the palace compound, the town was organized in eighty-six walled wards, each enclosing a population of 6,000–10,000 people with a total population of at least 600,000 people (density 10 dwelling units/ha.—referred to hereafter as DU/ha.). These wards were separated by extremely wide, straight avenues.[12] Each half of the town was served by vast wholesale markets. Changan served as a model for the layout of the eighth-century Japanese capital cities of Heijokyo (Nara) (Plate 4) and Heiankyo (Kyoto) (Plates 5, 6; Fig. 2). Only one fourth the size of Changan, Nara accommodated a population of some 200,000 people; Kyoto, about a third of the size of Changan, had a hierarchical layout consisting of sets and subsets on interrelated squares (see chapter 3), which still survives in the plan of the modern city.

In thirteenth-century Peking (the *Ta-Tu* or Khan-Balik of Kublai-Khan) the palace and administrative compound was moved back to the center as in the ancient Chou diagram.

Seoul, Korea, built in the fourteenth century, followed essentially the same system. A rectangle of 4×6 km.—it consisted of autonomous wards (*bang*). A census taken thirty-two years after the city's foundation gave the population as 103,328 persons in 16,921 households.[13]

India The plan of Mandalay, Burma, dating from 1857, proves that the Chinese model exerted its influence right up into the nineteenth century (Plate 7).

In India a rich literature developed concerning cosmological and practical rules for the layout of capital cities. A most interesting treatise on the subject—the *Silpasastra*—dates from the first millenium B.C. There is no evidence, however, of any Indian capital being built according to these rules, with the possible exception of Jaipur (1728 A.D.), which may also reflect European influence.

The various new capitals of the Moghul emperors show

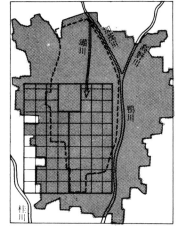

2 Plan of Heiankyo 794 A.D. (modern Kyoto) superimosed over modern built-up area.

little concern with overall planning. Fathpur-Sikri built by Akbar around 1573 A.D. is an example of splendid urban design, yet its site was selected by superstitious caprice and the town proved an economic failure to be abandoned after only fifteen years.

Persia Contemporary Isfahan was more of a success. In 1598 Shah Abbas moved the capital to Isfahan, which at the time had 40,000 inhabitants. Within thirty years the population grew tenfold to 400,000, a remarkable record. The new capital was built as a parallel city to the existing town, making use of local manpower. Innovative design in Isfahan focused on its central area, a vast complex of buildings around a formal square of 8 ha. which served both as a polo ground and market. The surrounding buildings contained government offices, caravanserai, bazaar, mosques, coffee houses, and public baths—a very modern activity-mix of civic, commercial, cultural, and leisure uses (Plate 8).

Europe In the Occident little was known of Far Eastern town planning. Medieval Europe produced no new capitals, and the first ideal plan for the residence of a prince may well be Filarete's Sforzinda. This plan (Plate 9) dates from 1464 and shows an eight-pointed star with eight radial avenues leading to gates and dividing the town into "borghi" each with its market, interconnected by a ringroad. A somewhat awkward rectangular palace complex takes up the center.

Practical experiments on a modest scale started with the rebuilding and expansion of existing settlements to adapt them to a more ambitious court function.[14] Among the first of these was the transformation of the village of Sabbioneta by Prince Vespasiano Gonzaga, whom Argan rightly praises for practicing "city planning as an art of government." Within a few years a new town rose on a rectangular street plan, equipped with a complete range of sociocultural institutions —school, library, museum, hospital, and the famous theater designed by Vincento Scamozzi.

Half a century later, between 1606 and 1620, Carlo di Gonzaga-Nevers, scion of the same enterprising family, built the first residence-town in France. The plan of Charleville is a rectangle with the "Place Ducal" as its center, framed by uniform buildings and dominated by the palace on its western side. The town is composed of four quadrants, each served by its market square. Plate 10 shows Charleville fifty years after its foundation (1656), already well equipped with hospitals, convents, asylums, and even a ball court.[15]

Another French residence, Richelieu, was founded in 1638 by the Cardinal of that name. The little rectangular town is juxtaposed to his palace and gardens; its interest lies in the architectural unity of its volumes, since uniform cornice lines and facades have been imposed on all buildings, foreshadowing Louis XIV's *ordonnances* for Versailles.

Versailles As a seminal event, one might also mention the decision of Philip II to move his court from Valladolid to the Escorial, built in 1563–84 on a virgin site. Although a building rather than a town, the Escorial combined palace and government functions and was admired by Louis XIV, who knew it through diplomatic and family connections. There seems to be a parallel here with Louis's idea to move his court and government from crowded Paris to create a new town around the hunting lodge of his father at Versailles. According to Lavedan, the first plan of the park-palace-and-town complex with its radiating avenues dates from 1665 and may have been the work of Le Nôtre. The actual foundation of the town did not take place, however, until 1671. Although work on the palace progressed rapidly and the court moved in 1682, only half of the town was built under Louis XIV. The second half, or "ville neuve" of Versailles was completed only under Louis XV. The proximity of Paris hindered the development of Versailles, and at the death of the Sun King, in 1717— after nearly fifty years of development—the population barely numbered 30,000. Even today the population of Versailles is far from reaching 100,000.

Great, however, has been the influence of the plan and spatial organization of Versailles: among the features which were widely imitated are the town *ordonnances* enforcing the uniform and harmonious appearance of all buildings, the "head" position of the palace to which the town appears subordinated, and the *patte d'oie* pattern of the three avenues converging at the entrance of the *cour d'honneur* (Plate 11). This formal device recurs in such residence towns as Karlskrona, Sweden (1680), Karlsruhe, Germany (1715), Aranjuez, Spain (1727), Bogorodsk, Russia (1778), and Tula, Russia (1779), as well as in the plans of the large capital cities of Washington and New Delhi. The plan of Versailles also had some influence on the development of St. Petersburg, the first new capital of modern times to grow into a great city.

St Petersburg The rise of the new Russian capital was due to the vision and ruthless energy of Peter I (1672–1725). His decision to transfer the government from Moscow was a commitment to a maritime and westward thrust of the empire. The new town was to serve as an instrument of his modernization policy. As of 1710 a building committee guided and regulated all construction. A special settlement district was assigned to each social class. Foreign architects were recruited and forced labor was drafted from all over Russia: to balance the population Peter ordered the migration of hundreds of families of nobles, merchants, and artisans. Of crucial importance was the early transfer of government functions from Moscow: the court as a whole moved in 1712, the diplomatic corps by 1718, and the judiciary in 1723.

A first master plan was produced in 1716 by the Italian Tressini, a second in 1717 by the Frenchman Leblond. Both plans (Plates 12a, b) concentrated development on Vasilievski

Island. Leblond's Baroque plan confined the town within oval fortifications. As Leblond died two years later, his plan was not executed,[16] and the new building director, Eropkin, convinced the czar to give priority to the development of the mainland rather than to the islands (Plate 12c).

Peter himself ordered the opening of an avenue on the south bank, leading from the Admirality tower straight to the important Novgorod-Moscow highway. This road—which later became the famous Nevski Prospekt—determined the direction of growth while the admirality complex became the germ of the developing town center. The tip of Vasilievski Island was reserved for cultural institutions (Plate 12c). At the time of Peter's death, the permanent population surpassed 40,000 persons. Peter's heirs sustained the development effort adhering to his original intentions.

In addition to naval yards and arsenals, industries were established producing a whole range of goods. By the nineteenth century St. Petersburg became the foremost industrial center of Russia. The population reached 200,000 persons in 1800, 400,000 in 1825, and 3 million inhabitants by 1900. Renamed Leningrad after the revolution the city lost its capital functions but remains the second largest metropolis of the USSR.

The creation and growth of St. Petersburg exemplify several important lessons:

— The personal identification of Peter and his successors, and their nearly unlimited power, helped to overcome all odds during the crucial early development phase.

— The early development of the city was rushed without regard to human and material cost. This created an irreversible commitment and the town achieved its "critical mass" before the death of its promoter.

— The creation of the capital was correctly used to further both national policy and modernization of society. The innovative and exemplary aspects of the town were given priority over welfare needs of the early residents.

— Peter recognized the need for a diversified employment base in addition to the governmental role of the capital: the establishment of educational and cultural institutions and of industry was encouraged from the start.

Washington D.C. In 1790 the Congress of the United States decided to create a new "national city" within a federal district of "no more than ten miles square." In 1792 President Washington appointed the French-born Major L'Enfant as town planner. Within a year he produced a master plan which was innovative in many respects:

L'Enfant had the audacity to propose a street plan covering 24,000 ha., at a time when the well-informed Jefferson considered 600 ha. more then sufficient. He had the vision to plan for at least 500,000 people at a time when the population of the new Russian capital barely passed 200,000 after eighty years of forced growth and when the prospereous American town of Boston had just reached a population of 18,000.[17]

The basic town structure proposed by L'Enfant consists of a generous web of diagonal avenues superimposed on the orthogonal grid of local streets (Plate 13). Yet L'Enfant did not start with a symbolic diagram or abstract geometry but from careful analysis of the topographic features of his site. He assigned the most prominent points to important buildings and connected them with straight avenues. In this, his goal was to assure easy legibility of the town structure by providing reciprocal views between the nodal buildings.

The main axis of his plan is Pennsylvania Avenue, leading from Georgetown past the White House to the Capitol, forming a *patte d'oie* pattern with Maryland Avenue and the 135 m. wide Mall.[18] Much has been made from the borrowing of this formal device to suggest L'Enfant derived his plan from Versailles, which he knew firsthand, yet the basic idea of interconnected nodes is more akin to the Renaissance urban design first used in the restructuring of Rome under Sixtus V.

Although the government moved to Washington as early as 1800 the city developed slowly. The Civil War finally made Washington the center of feverish activity. The abolition of slavery brought in the first great waves of Negro residents and shantytowns grew. This led in 1867 to a vast public works program under Commissioner Shepherd, who finally made a reality of L'Enfant's paper streets.

In spite of its initial implementation L'Enfant's plan was actually saved from neglect by the 1902 Senate Park Commission. Its members, including Daniel Burnham, McKim, and the younger Olmsted redefined the monumental core area of 350 ha. and proposed significant improvements for the development of its Potomac river edge. Their plan proved to be adaptable to changing land uses and for a period of fifty years adequately served increasing volumes of automobile traffic. Since 1950, however, the tidal commuting movement between suburbs and central-office employment imposed the construction of urban expressways and their alien geometry threatens the original plan with dismemberment.

Apart from its capital function, Washington is today a service center for the bicephalous Washington-Baltimore metropolitan area. Regional specialization permits Washington to grow without significant manufacturing employment, traditionally more oriented toward Baltimore.

In 1961 the "Year 2000 Plan" was published proposing a pattern for regional development along six radial corridors [19] where the creation of satellite towns was to be encouraged. This pattern would be weakened by the spontaneous ringlike growth generated along the new belt-parkway. But, in the inner city L'Enfant's plan still dominates and confirms Edmund Bacon's thesis that a forceful formal idea can achieve a momentum which will perpetuate itself through several generations. The originality of L'Enfant's plan is further proved by its radiation during the nineteenth century. The plans of various state capitals in the U.S.A. and elsewhere have been inspired by it: Indianapolis (1821), Madison, Wisconsin (1836), La Plata, Argentina (1883), and Belo Horizonte, Brazil (1895). Its continued influence can be easily traced in the twentieth-century national capitals of New Delhi, Canberra, and Brasilia.

New Delhi Around 1910 political considerations prompted the British to transfer the administration of the Indian Raj to the old Moghul capital of Delhi. A town planning committee proposed the creation of a new parallel town separated by a strip of parks from the native city of some 250,000 people.

Sir Edward Lutyens' Master Plan for New Delhi is based on the great east-west axis of Kingsway—1.5 miles long, with Government House on a hilltop at its western end, and as eastern counterpoint a large hexagonal space reserved for the palaces of the native princes. Kingsway forms the base of a triangle the northern point of which is the busy commercial node of Connaught Circle (Plate 14).

The planned area of New Delhi covers some 2,650 ha., yet growth beyond a population of 57,000 people was not contemplated as extremely low garden-city type density was envisaged. New Delhi was formally inaugurated in 1929. Ten years later the plan already seemed inadequate and the Delhi Development Committee was created to propose modifications, thus pointing up problems specific to wholly planned new towns in developing countries. Aspects of the formal plan exerted some influence on Canberra, and later on Chandigarh.

Canberra In Australia the federation of the six original colonies in 1900 created the need for a new national capital. An ambitious Master Plan by the Chicago architect Walter Burley Griffin was selected in 1912 (Plates 15, 16) but its implementation was slow. Parliament only transferred there in 1921 and until recently much of the administration remained anchored in other cities.

The main feature of Griffin's plan was the creation of a series of lakes by damming the flood plain of the frequently dry Monongolo River. A crystalline pattern of streets and avenues was to be superimposed on the surrounding hills. The monumental aspects of Griffin's plan are related to Lutyens' plan for New Delhi. Central to his scheme was the triangle formed by two mile-long avenues connecting functionally distinct sectors clustered around the capitol, the city hall, and the main railroad station (Plate 17).

In 1957 the National Development Corporation started work and by 1964 the six-and-a-half square-mile pleasure lake with its barrage and bridges was completed. Population influx stimulated by the building activity has become rapid (Plates 18a, b).[20] Heavy industry is not considered compatible with the primary functions of the city, but light manufacturing and research establishments are encouraged to locate in the capital area. The increasing importance of Canberra as a national educational and cultural center further increases its pull. With its fairly homogeneous and high-income population, Canberra is free of the numerous social problems plaguing other new capitals and has the potential to grow into a large city while maintaining its good environmental quality.[21]

The recent creation of a national park in the vicinity of Canberra adds greatly to the attractions of the capital, which Lord Holford rightly called a place "to retire to rather than from."

Latin America In Latin America some of the colonial towns were planned with a very large area and were destined to be capitals of various importance within the colonial empire (e.g., Lima: founded in 1545, with the stated aim to serve as "Corte y Capital del Reino del Peru"). The nineteenth century contributed the foundation of two important regional capitals: La Plata in the Argentine and Belo Horizonte in Brazil.

La Plata was founded in 1883. The plan is a perfect square of 600 ha. crossed by diagonals (Plate 19).

Belo Horizonte was created a few years later than La Plata to replace the mining town of Ouro Preto as capital of Minas Gerais State. The planned area covered 1,200 ha. limited by a ring boulevard. The layout consisted of a small-scale orthogonal grid with superimposed on it a diagonal supergrid of avenues that were to accomodate electric trolley lines (Plate 20).

Finally, 1932 marks the foundation of Goiania, capital of the state of Goias, in Brazil. Planned for a modest population with a garden-city layout, the town very rapidly outgrew its target size. The foundations of Belo Horizonte and of Goiania represent important antecedents to the creation of Brasilia; the rapid growth rate of these towns served as a warning to the planners of Brasilia not to underestimate the growth potential of the new capital.

Brasilia The dramatic rise of Brasilia has been described as "madness but heroic madness." The sixth largest nation in the world built its new capital with unprecedented speed.

The main incentive for locating the new capital in the empty heartland of Brasil was the need for a "growth pole" of development to pull settlement toward the interior. Already the first republican constitution of 1891 foresaw the reservation of a 14,400 km. square area for the future capital, and the new constitution of 1946 decreed the designation of a Federal District of 5,000 km. square on the plateau of Goias.

The actual site was pinpointed by the American firm of Donald J. Belcher in 1954; following this President Kubitschek created in 1956 NOVACAP the development corporation for the new town. Lucio Costa's now famous plan was presented and accepted in 1957.

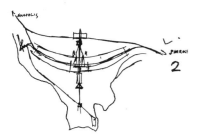

2

3 Brasilia ideogram
sketches by Lucio Costa.

Reviewing the twenty-five projects submitted in national competition for the plan of Brasilia, there can be little doubt that Costa's plan was superior to the rest, all of which seem to lack unity of conception.[22] Perhaps the best alternative proposal was the project of the Roberto brothers: a poly-nuclear metropolis formed by hexagonal clusters of 72,000 inhabitants of about five km. diameter and with overall densities of forty persons per hectare (Plate 23). By contrast, Costa's famous plan is of diagrammatic clarity. It is formed by two great axes shaped like a bow spanned by an arrow. The bow-shaped seventeen-km.-long residential axis is crossed in its middle by a straight east-west monumental axis (Fig. 3). A vast traffic interchange and bus terminal is the heart of the plan. Toward east the three-and-a-half-km.-long mall leads to the "Plaza of the Three Powers," with its monumental group of government buildings—the same axis toward the west is accented by a television tower, and leads to a municipal plaza and beyond it to the railroad station. A third avenue (corresponding to the string of the bow) serves warehousing and light industrial areas.

Work started immediately, with the architect Niemeyer in charge of the design of all public buildings. Construction workers erected the "Cidade Livre," a shantytown with frontier flavor (by 1959 it had a population of about 64,000, of which only one third was female!). The disorderly growth and size of Cidade Livre soon raised the problem of how to accomodate future waves of migrants, and in 1958 the decision was made to prepare reception areas in the form of satellite towns at distances of 25–70 km. from the center of Brasilia. This decision contributed to making Brasilia into a stratified city, expressing overt class distinction. Low-income and marginal families now live in the satellites; lesser civil servants and employees in rowhouses and walkups on the east side of the curved axis; middle-income employees in elegant elevator apartments on the west side of the same axis; while diplomats and the rich reside in villas along the shoreline of the lake (Plates 21a, b).

On 21 April 1960 the city was officially inaugurated. Although President Kubitschek soon lost control, succeeding governments maintained program continuity and the building of Brasilia slowed down but did not stop. In 1965 the Medici Government ordered the transfer of 35,000 government employees and their families, and on the tenth anniversary of the inauguration cabinet ministers were instructed to conduct all government business in Brasilia. The diplomatic corps completed its move from Rio by 1972. By 1970 Brasilia had a population of half a million, about evenly divided between the inhabitants of the "formal" city and the satellite settlements (Plates 22a, b). The city was planned for the scale and speed of the automobile and with its vast distances and openness is not actually a very pleasant environment for pedestrians.

Chandigarh The partition of India in 1947 led to the foundation of two cities: Chandigarh—"the fortress of the war goddess"—new capital of the Indian State of Punjab and Islamabad—"the city of Islam"—new capital of Pakistan. Chandigarh was the first to get started: a new administrative center was needed since Lahore, the traditional capital of the Punjab, was awarded to Pakistan.

In 1950 the Indian Government invited the American planner, Albert Mayer, and the architect, Matthew Novicki, to prepare a Master Plan. Mayer proposed a town structure accommodating half a million people. He placed the capitol area in a "head position" toward the north and organized the town in large neighborhoods divided by gently curved major east-west roads (Plate 24). In 1951 Novicki died in an airplane accident. The government turned, for reasons of international exchange, to Le Corbusier and the English architects Maxwell Fry and Jane Drew for further elaboration of the plan.

Prime Minister Jawaharlal Nehru, who took great interest in the project, instructed Le Corbusier to build a "new town . . . unfettered by the traditions of the past, an expression of the nation's future."

Le Corbusier saw in the planning task an opportunity to test his theories of urban order. He did not alter, but merely rectified, the basic concept of the Mayer plan. He imposed a strict hierarchy of roads—his famous "seven V" system— ranging from expressways to bicycle paths, and he defined the basic cellular unit of the town, as rectangular sectors of $800 \times 1,200$m. or roughly one km. square.

The "sector" is essentially an introverted neighborhood confined by V3 grid roads. Vehicular traffic can penetrate the sector only at midpoints of the N-S avenues. Pedestrian strips form a continuous path system, crossing the grid road at bus stops (Plate 25). The sectors are designed for low densities varying from 50–100 persons per ha., or 5,000– 10,000 persons per sector. Within the blocks one finds considerable segregation by income since government employees receive lots assigned to them by the hierarchical rank they occupy in the administration.

Each sector is equipped with a primary and a secondary school, a service center and some 20–50 shops aligned along the shady south side of the E-W distributor street. These commercial strips generate much animation, in contrast to the town center in sector 17 that opened in 1960 and which groups movies, library, town hall, banks around a vast unshaded plaza alien to Indian tradition; it is perhaps the least successful element of the Corbusian city.

Corbusier's pilot project was accepted in 1951. Implementation started immediately at several distant nodes: the capital area, the southwestern sector, and the university area.

The showpiece of Chandigarh is the capitol with the great sculptural buildings designed by Le Corbusier (Plate 26). In Chandigarh the government employs every second active person, and the jobs are concentrated in the capitol area far removed from the residential sectors. The favored means of transportation is the bicycle, but the big distances sap the energy of the pedaling commuters. The city has achieved some importance as an educational and cultural center. It is less successful as a commercial center and its regional impact has been negligible. In 1968 industrial employment accounted for only 9 percent of all jobs. Considering that taxation has been waived for twenty-five years to encourage the growth of the city, the results are disappointing. Chandigarh suffers from overplanning and strict controls. It has no self-government and is considered by Indians to be an expensive city to live in. Little attempt has been made to make it attractive for marginal population groups.

The overall plan of Chandigarh is of ageless dignity: yet it has little in common with Indian tradition and rather curiously resembles plans of Chinese capital cities, notably of Changan. Designed rather than planned, the town is a monument to the artistic genius of Le Corbusier: it is also a mirage which does not quite fit in with Indian reality and it is doubtful whether it can mold the Indian of the future.

Islamabad The idea of building Islamabad originated in 1959. By that time the population of Brasilia was fast approaching the 100,000 mark and the building of Chandigarh also had attracted world-wide attention. The need for a new administrative center had been obvious since the partition: Lahore, the traditional capital, was too close to the Indian border; the congested port city of Karachi was inadequate as a permanent capital.

Regional planning was assigned to Sir Robert Matthew, who selected a site at the foot of a range of hills in a cool climate with plentiful water and good brick earth. Sir Robert insisted that to justify the vast expenditure in such a poor country the new capital must also play a regional role and act as a growth pole for the industrialization of north Pakistan.

The nearby town of Rawalpindi was to be considered not just as a source of labor during the construction phase of the new town but as a complementary twin city of Islamabad. Cultural and administrative functions of national scope would be centered in Islamabad while Rawalpindi would grow in importance as a regional commercial and industrial center.

A planning district of no less then 64,000 ha. was designated which includes the reservation for a national park. Within the district, the Islamabad-Rawalpindi metropolitan area occupies some 25,000 ha. A Capital Development Authority, created in 1963, attempts to bring the entire planning area under public ownership. The preparation of a Master Plan was assigned to C. Doxiades Associates (Plate 27). Careful evaluation of the experience at Brasilia and Chandigarh permitted Doxiades to develop a plan which is far more rational then the more artistically inspired designs of Costa and Le Corbusier.

The form proposed for the city of Islamabad is an elongated triangle wedged between the east-west range of Murgala Hills. The agglomeration of Rawalpindi will be contained within the grid of four highways (Plate 28). The government center is placed at the tip of the triangle, terminating the perspective along the main axis of the town, which parallels the hill range. This capitol area is surrounded by a special housing precinct assigned to diplomats and members of the parliament (Plate 29).

The town, organized according to a rigorous functional hierarchy, is composed of rectangular sectors twice as large as in Chandigarh and four times larger then the neighborhood unit of Brasilia. These "Class V"-type communities are confined between arterial roads 2,200 m.-on-center with 400 m. wide right-of-ways. The enclosed area of 324 ha. will serve a population of 20–40,000 people, with average gross densities of around 100 persons per ha (Plate 30). Each sector will be practically a self-contained town with its own center, and employment possibilities offered in offices and in workshops for crafts and light industries. These large sectors are divided into three or four subcommunities of "Class IV" and these again are composed of the basic village-size planning units for some 2,000 people. In keeping with Doxiades' concept of dynamic growth (Dynapolis), all citywide activities are grouped along linear spines capable of gradual extension. A separate spine is proposed for Islamabad and for Rawalpindi with southwesterly growth indicated for both (Plate 27). The diversified employment base and the rational and efficient town structure seem to guarantee rapid growth for Islamabad, which more than Brasilia and Chandigarh seems to provide an adequate model for capital building in a developing country.

Conclusions

The rapid growth of some capital cities was often due to the personal identification of a ruler or head of state with the project. To ensure the exemplary and modernizing impact of the capital the best talent was recruited—if necessary from abroad. Until the present century the designers of new capitals were preoccupied with monumental aspects of the town structure and the geometric relation of the street pattern to public buildings. By contrast, the hierarchical planning of twentieth-century capitals is dominated by traffic considerations and concern with the scale of residential areas.

Little attention has been paid to social planning so far. Yet the example of Washington proves that new capitals become magnets for minority and marginal groups. In multiracial societies and nations with uneven levels of development between regions, marginal groups rush to the capital to profit from its superior welfare services, while minorities are attracted by the more tolerant atmosphere and the hope of getting on the government payroll. Whether desired or not, capital cities have a "melting pot" vocation and must integrate disadvantaged groups into the mainstream of national life. The physical structure of the city should serve this social planning objective; so far, however, hierarchical planning has created de facto segregation by housing patterns based on income, thus perpetuating class barriers.

Capital cities must be exemplary in their physical planning and set standards by the quality and quantity of their equipment. A Master Plan prepared for a fixed town size will assure an orderly and efficient town structure once the target population level has been reached. However, adherence to the Master Plan may require the deliberate neglect of initial concentration and efficiency, putting great stress and discomfort on the early residents who become indeed a "sacrificed generation." Dynamic town models providing for efficiency in function of time with a town structure capable of balanced growth offer a solution to this dilemma: in this the Dynapolis concept of Doxiades may point the way (Plate 27).

Although each new capital is unique we may derive some generalizations from our study:

— New capitals prove that very large towns can be built rapidly according to a comprehensive plan—even by developing countries suffering both from a lack of financial and staff resources. Such success is encouraging the trend toward ever-larger scale for the new towns planned to restructure or to decongest existing conurbations. (See chapter 5)

— The fact that some capital cities thrive on tertiary employment furnishes an argument against the imperative of an industrial base and toward new towns based on employment provided by education, research, or entertainment activities.

— The examples of Washington and of Canberra prove that in countries with multi-party governments—where the "democratic process" hampers the implementation of any great concept—it is nevertheless possible to maintain program continuity and adhere to the plan, a. if the original design has sufficient symbolic content to impose itself on subsequent decision makers and b. if the heavy initial investment creates an "irreversible commitment."

The above considerations focus attention on the consensus and pride-building function of symbolic structures, justifying a strategy of "let's do the inessentials first, the essentials will follow. . . ."

3 COLONIAL TOWNS

Definitions

The proliferation of colonial towns has been of tremendous importance to worldwide urbanization. An overwhelming number of towns in both Americas, in South Africa, Australia, and Siberia are of colonial origin, as well as some of the most important ports and trade centers of south and southeast Asia and Africa. The primary purpose of colonization is the exploitation of location-bound human and natural resources; the secondary objective is decongestion by migration which permits the maintainance of a certain demographic and ecological balance in the metropolis.

We will distinguish here between external and internal colonization. *External colonization* is directed by a parent state toward lands outside its boundaries and generally involves the settlement of colonists on territory already claimed by an autochthonous population. *Internal colonization* is a development policy of states with large unevenly settled regions to create a more balanced population distribution in order to make more effective use of all resources within the limits of the national territory. A modern example of systematic internal colonization is the policy of the Soviet Union to urbanize its Asiatic territories.

According to their origins, the colonial towns can be grouped in five categories:

1 *Agro-military settlements* have the function of securing a contested frontier and to signal the intention of the colonizing power to maintain a permanent presence. Such were the Roman veteran settlements, the medieval "bastides," the first wave of the Hispanic *poblaciones* in America, or the nineteenth century settlements of French colons in Algeria.

2 *Trade Centers* are mostly port cities since their primary function is to maintain communications with the parent state and to act as collecting and shipping points for export goods and as distribution points for imports from the metropolis. These towns were "extraverted" and were frequently fortified because of their strategic importance, resulting in core cities of fairly high densities.

3 *Regional Centers* are more "introverted" towns serving as markets, administrative, and service centers of their area. Created in a second phase of colonization in the interior of an already stabilized colony, they do not require fortifications and consequently can spread out more leisurely at low densities.

4 *Mining and industrial towns:* some colonial mining towns like Potosí (Bolivia), grew rapidly to large size, yet until the late nineteenth century such towns were unplanned and grew in disorder around the plant or mine. Modern industrial towns are frequently used as "growth poles" in developing regions and as key elements of internal colonization. Because of their importance they will be discussed separately (See chapter 4).

5 *New Towns* founded on *artificially created land* are a special case of internal colonization. Such towns are most often located on new land gained by land-reclamation methods; in some cases they may be built on artificial islands above underwater sources of oil or coal like Gunkajima in Nagasaki Bay, Japan.

Large-scale land reclamation can also serve as the vehicle for internal colonization:

In 1930 Mussolini ordered the draining of the Pontine marshes in central Italy and the creation of five model settlements. The town of Littoria (now Latina) is the administrative center for the region.

About the same time, the Dutch engaged in the more ambitious scheme of reclaiming 225,000 ha. of land from the Zuider Zee. By 1932 the main dike was completed and work started on the four large polders. The settlement system proposed for the region is based on villages serving about 90 sq. km. of farmland with a population of 3,000.

Towns of about 30,000 population will provide essential services to the villages of each polder. So far, Emmeloord, center of the Nordestpolder and Dronten, in Est Flevoland, show fast growth. The capital of the entire region will be Lelystad, with a population of 100,000. The plan, commissioned from the architect C. van Eesteren in 1958, consists of sectors formed by roads 1.5 km. on center. These roads are elevated 7 m. with secondary streets passing below them on a lower level. This system of traffic separation permits unhindered access of pedestrians and bicycles to the center (Plates 31, 32). Another town of the 100,000 size, Almere (or Pampus) is proposed halfway between Lelystad and Amsterdam, corresponding to an urbanization axis along the shoreline of the Flevoland polders.

The origins and spread of the grid plan

Throughout history the use of the grid-type street pattern has been a distinctive trademark of colonial towns. Since this study is concerned with the evolution of planning ideas, we shall examine briefly the origins and spread of the ubiquitous grid.

Much ink has been spilt in trying to derive the origins of the grid plan from a single source. It is relatively easy to trace the ancestry of the Western street-grid from Roman, Hellenistic, Greek, and even Assyrian practice. An exchange of ideas between ancient Egypt, Mesopotamia, and the Indus valley civilization is admitted and accounts perhaps for the enigmatic regularity of Mohenjo Daro.[1]

It is less easy to explain widespread use of the grid in the China of the Chou dynasty (1123–256 B.C.), and even less the fact that characters scratched on oracle bones dating from the Shang dynasty (1765–1123 B.C.) already imply a hierarchy of rectangular walled cities.[2]

There can be no doubt that the grid pattern was also used in pre-Columbian America: apart from its use by the fifteenth-century Inca empire [3] there is also proof that land reclamation methods used in the extensions of Tenochtitlan-Mexico resulted in a regular grid pattern [4] and that the ancient city of Teotihuacan gradually developed from axiality through orthogonality toward a grid system in the strict sense of the word.

Axiality, the use of straight processionals, or even of a street-cross does not by itself prove the existence of a planned grid. Religious importance accorded to orientation of the cardinal points often resulted in the juxtaposition of rectangular elements (Changan, Angkor) without leading to a grid-system; the open space left between the built areas is a separation rather than a movement system. More than just an orthogonal pattern, the grid is formed by the intersection of two series of parallel lines and implies a priority accorded to the public movement system. Grid planning is efficiency maximizing; it is the opposite of welfare-oriented planning based on the cell (the individual, the family or the neighborhood).

I am inclined to believe that the grid pattern is discovered spontaneously by any civilization having reached a certain maturity in its evolution. Certain agricultural patterns—irrigation, land reclamation—almost inevitably lead to the use of the efficient grid pattern. All countries using large scale irrigation methods seem to have discovered it: Mesopotamia, Indus Valley, Egypt, China, and the Pacific coast of ancient Peru.

Furthermore, the grid pattern can also derive from the order and discipline of military organization. Any army that is capable of marching in lockstep and orderly columns would almost certainly muster and form battle arrays in orderly rectangles and encamp in the same form. This includes the Assyrians, Chinese, Hellenes, Romans, Incas, and the Khmer. Logistics and the need for pitching tents according to rank and corps early attracted theoretical attention, and was developed by the Romans into the art of *castrametatio,* the direct ancestor of rational planning.

Once discovered, the advantages of the grid are manifold: it is by far the simplest system for surveying and subdividing land, and one that is easily implemented with the help of rope and ruler even by the most uncouth soldier or colonist. It also lends itself to easy record keeping—facilitating census taking and taxation, the favored means of governments trying to keep track of their far-flung colonial subjects. The ease of record keeping also helps transactions of property and land speculation in societies where private property can be held and exchanged. Finally a town grid makes orientation easy for strangers, and it is a pleasant pattern for small and medium towns. It only becomes unbearably monotonous if endlessly spread over large areas. The popularity of the grid encouraged the choice of flat sites where the pattern is easiest to apply, yet on occasion the grid has been stretched over steep grades and resulted in such exhilarating urban landscapes as Priene and San Francisco.

Although these considerations seem self-evident it is important to recall the ubiquitous use of the grid by civilizations separated by time and space, which seems to contradict the notion of the town structure as an ideogram of the economic organization and cultural values of a society.

Historical survey

Near East, Greece, Rome Let us now cast a glance at the archeological and historical evidence:

In the ancient Near East the Assyrians may have been the first to make systematic use of the foundation of towns to consolidate their conquest. Frankfort claims [5] that their new towns were based on the grid pattern, although the evidence is still scanty. We know that the eighth century B.C. Urartian town of Zernaki Tepe was laid out in a perfect checkerboard (Plate 33).[6]

Recently, aerial photography and excavations have proved that Greek colonies in southern Italy and Sicily used grid-type layouts as early as the seventh century B.C.; hence Aristotle must have been wrong in crediting Hippodamus of Miletus with the invention of the pattern.[7] However, Hippodamus was certainly among the first international planning consultants whose name has come down to us. He may have been the first to introduce the new style in Attica, together with other outlandish innovations like the closed Milesian Agora lined with shops on three sides.

The fact is that most Ionian cities destroyed during the Persian wars were rebuilt according to the "neóteros trópos" or new style—and this pattern has also become the trademark of the post-war Greek colonies which accompanied a great upswing in international trade. Miletus, which gave the name to the Greek grid, was itself a large colonizing center which reputedly founded sixty new urban nuclei (Plate 34).

The pattern became an important tool of urbanization in the hands of Alexander of Macedon and his successors, the Diadochi. In eleven years Alexander founded at least thirteen towns bearing his name and his diligent heirs started some seventy more [8] during the following twenty-two years. The Seleucids were responsible for thirty-five of them and they were no mean towns: Seleucia covered 300 ha., a rectangle of 2100m. × 1500m. The town of Dura-Europos, founded about 300 B.C.—where Macedonian veterans were settled—sported block sizes of 70.5m. × 35.2m. with street widths of 7m. and 8m. and an avenue of 12m.—which would still make a good plan today (Fig. 4).

According to Wycherley [9] the Seleucids developed a standard plan for easy reuse; similarly, nineteenth-century Amer-

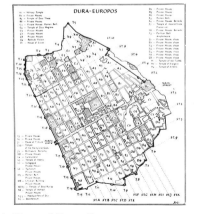

4 Plan of Dura-Europos
c. 300 B.C.

ican railroad companies like the Illinois Central used the same plat to lay out 33 new towns along its tracks around 1885.

The influence of Hellenistic planning on the evolution of the Roman colonial town is well documented.

The Roman *colonia* developed from the organization of the prototypical military camp or *castrum,* which reflects the military ritual of Roman troops drawn up for review. Assuming the position of the duty officer facing the east, the north-south position of his shoulders would define the axis of the principal avenue or *Cardo* and the avenue in front of him would be the *Decumanus* leading to the main gate or *Porta Praetoria.* To the west of the crossing point the two axes would be the *Forum* surrounded by the camp squares marked out for the cohorts. As solid walls and building blocks replaced the tents and palisades the camp gradually became a permanent garrison town. According to Polybius the castrum plan derived from the model of the Hellenistic towns with their characteristic cross of two avenues. On the other hand Frontinus asserts that the pattern was directly copied from Pyrrhus' camp which the Romans captured intact at Beneventum in 275 B.C.[10]

The foundation of colonial settlements began under the Roman Republic, first in Italy and then in Iberia. Veteran colonies were settled in Naples, Bologna, Parma, and Piacenza, followed by Como, Pavia, Verona, Aosta. These towns were planned for a target population of perhaps 30,000— i.e., Piacenza and Cremona were both settled with 6,000 families. The grid blocks—generally of 80 m. (250 ft.) side-length—are still preserved in the structure of modern towns like Torino or Verona.

Augustus and his successors pursued a colonization policy coordinated with the extension of the highway network of the empire. Garrison towns of impressive uniformity were founded in Austria (Carnuntum), England (Chester), or Africa (Lambaesis) with sizes of 10–25 ha. Colonies for veterans like Aosta or Turin were larger—40–50 ha.—and civilian colonies like Cologne reached 100 ha. During the later empire the geometry of the colonial town was sometimes imposed on the surrounding countryside to form a regional grid for land allocation. The imprint of this "centuriatio" is still visible from the air in the Po Valley, Dalmatia, and North Africa.[11] This geometrization of the land resembles the Chinese regional grid of the Chou and the later continental checkerboard of the 1785 U.S. Land Ordinance.

An elaborate foundation act established the legal existence of the Roman colony, preceding any construction. The rectangular limitation of the town was of religious significance to the Romans as it was to the Chinese. However, the Romans never devised a mechanism for orderly expansion and once the town area filled up, suburbs developed at random outside of the walls, as can be seen on the aerial photographs of the remnants of Timgad (Thamugadi, Fig. 5; Plate 35).

5 Plan of Timgad c. 100 A.D.

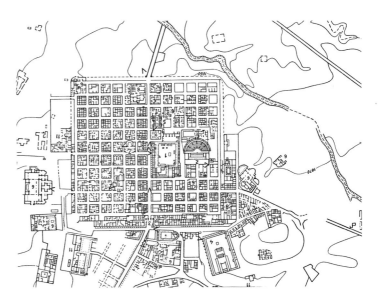

The great achievement of Roman planning was the development of the concept of the minimum adequate equipment of a town related to the number of its inhabitants. No new town was considered complete without a full range of public buildings and amenities: aqueducts, baths, fora, theaters, stadia. The prestige of the town depended on these outward signs of wealth and imperial favor, with the result that Roman towns surpassed our modern cities in the provision of fresh water or in the seating capacity of their theaters and stadia, and in some cases even in the supply of water per head of population.

China In China the forging of a feudal empire by the Chou dynasty (1123–256 B.C.) led to internal colonization. A new regional system of settlements was imposed upon the country with the help of orthogonal land-planning methods. This early use of the geometrical pattern could have been derived from irrigation and flood prevention techniques as well as from philosophical and cosmological speculation, such as the desire to establish harmony between the order of the universe and the man-made environment.

Since Chinese cosmology did not picture the world as circular but rather as an infinite series of lines parallel to the cardinal directions—defining sets of concentric rectangles—it seemed appropriate to reflect this concept in the spatial organization of the empire. Further, the Confucian ideal of social hierarchy led to the development of the concept of a minimum adequate spatial standard according to the cast and rank of the individual. The results can be exemplified by the "tsing-tien" land planning system advocated by Meng-Tse (371–288 B.C.): all land was to be divided into sections of one li (about 530 m. or 1600 ft.) square; the section was to be subdivided further in the form of the character "tsing" (#) into nine equal squares or Fu and each of these squares into 100 (10 × 10) lots, or Mo. The eight peripheral lots of the section were each assigned to a peasant family and the eight families were collectively responsible for the cultivation of the central ninth lot which belonged to the state.[12]

Rural areas were to be administered from small service towns or Cheng—1 li square in size accommodating 2,000–3,000 people. Such towns were surrounded by a double wall: the area between the walls was used by the peasants and their cattle in time of danger and served as expansion space for the town. Once this outer ring was built up the town would be reclassified as a Yi or regional center (up to 15,000 people) which by repeating the same growth process could gain the rank of a Tu or provincial capital (Plate 36).[13] The internal organization of the town was guided by the concept of minimum adequate size and the structure of Shu society which consisted of four classes: the Shih—an elite group like the Japanese samurai, considered morally superior—and farmers, artisans, and merchants.

Residential areas of the same class were grouped into village-sized Fangs surrounded by their own walls and penetrated by only four gates. Within the walls, the ward population formed a military-economic cooperative group.

Kung Fu Tse defines the optimum size Fang as consisting of 625 families, or about 3,000 people:

— five families form a cluster

— five clusters a group

— five groups a neighborhood

— five neighborhoods a village or urban ward, i.e., a Fang.[14]

Taking account of the larger households of the Shih, the net density of a Fang may have been around 100 persons per ha., with the wards of the other classes having densities up to 400 persons per ha. Strict zoning was used: each Fang was equipped with its own enclosed market, temple, and administration buildings. In addition, each town had one or two large wholesale markets and a government district with its palace. A hierarchy of roads was also introduced. Fast (imperial) and local traffic lanes were distinguished, it was even proposed to provide separate lanes for men and for women.

The extreme rationality of space allocation indicates that population densities must have been already considerable, and urban space scarce, as early as Chou China. Compared to Hellenistic or Roman colonization the contemporary Chinese planning of the Chou was more advanced in its concept of the functional cellular unit as a subset of the larger town plan, and in having devised a mechanism ensuring orderly town expansion within the matching grid of the town and its region.[15]

Europe The Chinese achievements of internal colonization were, of course, quite unknown in medieval Europe where even the principles of Roman town planning had been forgotten. "Above all it must be made clear," states the historian Paul Hofer, "that the surviving Roman towns had long been saturated beyond recognition by ever denser medieval sediment: their street system erased, their remnants built upon or overgrown." [16] Yet the art of formal planning survived in the layout of monasteries. The ninth-century ideal plan of a monastery preserved in St. Gall (Plate 37) gives a good idea of the complex functional relationships. In fact, monasteries were economically self-contained new communities (albeit of incomplete age/sex mix) housing, in some cases, over a thousand persons and acting at the same time as centers of learning, hostels, hospitals, and as agro-industrial combines engaging in the large-scale production of consumer and luxury goods (beer, cheese, parchment, linen, etc.). Monasteries not only provided training in planning and in the coordination of large-scale building operations but often participated actively in new town ventures (See in particular below on colonial towns in Latin America).

In addition, works on castrametation survived in the courts of the more erudite *seigneurs* and may have provided a source of inspiration when new town building once more became the fashion in the twelfth century. By that time an expanding rural population provided a "push factor" for *external colonization:* increased efforts were made to reconquer Spain from the Moors by the stepwise establishment of agro-military settlements (*repoblación concejil*) and in 1147 A.D. the Wendish crusade marked the beginning of the "Ostpolitik" of Henry the Lion (Duke of Saxony and Bavaria) and the penetration of Slavic lands by German colonists building new towns on a scale unsurpassed elsewhere in medieval Europe.

Efforts at *internal colonization* were triggered by the reawakening of the communal form of urban organization during the eleventh century in the Rhineland, the Low Countries, and in Northern Italy—adding a third force to the established powers of the church and the feudal families.[17]

Threatened by the rising economic and military power of the cities, secular and spiritual lords tried to maintain their position by implanting new towns in their own domains. At the same time the emerging money-economy forced the *seigneurs* to look for new sources of cash income, which they found in the rents and custom duties that could be levied in new market towns.

Such new towns were founded by kings, bishops, or dukes individually, or as "paréages" or joint ventures: the local lord providing the site, with the king guaranteeing privileges and protection. New settlers were recruited by a "locator" or "poblador" mostly among the subjects of the promoter, but in some cases also from foreign countries. Thus Frenchmen were frequently recruited for settlement in Spain, while German settlers were much in demand by Polish, Czech, and Hungarian kings.[18]

Due to such plantations during the twelfth century, the number of towns in central and in northern Europe doubled. Stimulated by their success, and perhaps to some extent by St. Thomas Aquinas' exhortations that the founding of towns was a special duty of the Christian Prince,[19] an unprecedented "new town boom" occurred during the thirteenth century; the number of German towns grew tenfold, the number of Swiss towns quintupled.[20]

If many of the foundations were "get-rich-quick" schemes with whimsical site selection, some serious attempts were also made toward town-plantation in a *regional context:* the twelfth-century Dukes of Zähringen were first to recognize that a chain of new towns could serve their dynastic policy. Their fifteen new towns served the strategy of forging a new state straddling the Rhine and uniting possessions in south Germany with what is now Switzerland (1120–1190). Somewhat later Edward I "rex et bastidor," King of England and Wales and Duke of Gascony, pursued a new town policy of truly international scope.

Some plantations had a primarily *military function:* among them the towns planted by Edward I in recently subdued Wales. However it would be misleading to state that new towns in general were "mainly military bastions" and that "walls were the first thing built by the colonists." [21] On the contrary both Beresford and Hofer insist that in many cases the walls were built with a delay of a century after the foundation—although the settlers clamored for walls both as a status symbol and as a protection against unruly neighbors.[22] (Among Zähringian towns, Murten, founded in 1179, received its walls in 1238; Rottweil, founded in 1150, had to wait for its walls until 1241.)

On the basis of this evidence one might argue that *economic objectives* dominated military considerations in the inception of medieval new towns. Thus Beresford sees the prime reason for the proliferation of "bastides" in thirteenth-century Gascony to be the greatly increased demand for claret wine for exportation.

The economic motivation is clearly imprinted on the plan of most medieval foundations in the importance given to the location and size of the market, regardless of the details of the internal disposition. By contrast, the parish churches generally occupy a secondary, lateral location.

Although the layout of the medieval new towns was often dictated by the topography, orthogonal grid plans form an impressive group.[23]

Checkerboard layouts with large central market squares predominate in the Germanic borderlands (Wiener-Neustadt, 1194; Neu Brandenburg, 1248; Retz, 1275; also Wohlau, Oschatz, Gleiwitz, Hamm, Bruck, Leoben, Budweis, Wroclav, etc.) as in the Anglo-French "bastides." Rectangular grids with elongated blocks range from Apulia [24] (Manfredonia, 1256; Cittaducale, 1309, etc.) to Gascony (Monpazier, 1284).

Checkerboard plans with central market squares proved

economically vulnerable, however, since the market—on which the town's revenues depended—was confined between the most substantial buildings and hence could not easily expand.

A successful deviation from the central market square was the linear market spine introduced in the Zähringian foundations, most strikingly in Bern where the market grew in proportion to the successive extensions of the town.[25] In an aerial photograph of modern Bern (Plate 38)—the original market spine and its successive extensions are clearly legible. This linear growth model has great similarity to such modern concepts as Doxiades' Dynapolis or the plan of the town of Hook (Plates 86, 87).

In general, the modular planning unit of medieval new towns has been the *homestead* or "platea" which served as basis for the calculation of the rent rolls. A foundation with 50–70 original homesteads was considered largely adequate although it implies an initial group of 250 to 500 settlers at most.

Since one of the privileges of a citizen in a new "liber burgus" was the freedom to give, sell, or mortgage his house and land, the "plateae" soon became subdivided into smaller burgage plots. Based on the rents paid, the population of these towns can be estimated: it rarely passed the level of 3,000 by the end of the fourteenth century. It is manifest that medieval plantations were rather smaller than Roman garrison towns—generally less than ten hectares. Zähringian Murten for example was a rectangle of 255m. × 155m. (only 3.5 ha.).

In general one might state that the twelfth-century foundations proved more successful than the much more numerous new towns of the thirteenth century. Towns with a primarily defense role remained small or atrophied; by contrast many market towns and ports prospered and some grew into important cities: Lübeck, 1158; Freiburg, 1120; Leipzig, 1180; Bern, 1190; Hull, 1293.

Eventually the thirteenth-century new town "boom" led to hypertrophy and stagnation. The number of fourteenth-century plantations is markedly less numerous. The Black Death of 1349 and the resulting decimation of the population put a temporary end to the formation of new communities, and attention shifted to the restructuring and enlargement of existing centers.

The growing importance of artillery during the fifteenth century led to great interest in the art of fortifications. An abundant crop of "ideal" proposals resulted in which more ingenuity was lavished on the design of the defenses than on the town structure within.[26]

A new profession of fortification- and town-planner developed in Italy and these roving consultants spread the latest fashions around the globe. Among the first we find Girolamo Marini laying out the town of Vitry-le-François (1545); yet at the same time his compatriot Giovanni Battista Antonelli is already in the Spanish Indies, tracing the plan of Antigua (Guatemala) and building the bastions of Cartagena. In the second half of the sixteenth century some fortress towns were built on a starshape pattern with radiating avenues, as Philippeville (1555), Coeworden (1597), and Palmanova (1593). This inefficient pattern was soon abandoned and the checkerboard prevailed even within the limits of polygonal fortifications.[27] Although numerous garrison towns were built, none has grown large: Palmanova, which was planned for 20,000 people never accomodated more than 5,000.[28] Although innovative in many respects, the importance of new town building in sixteenth-century Europe pales in comparison with the scope of the urbanization effort in Latin America—discussed in the following section. During the seventeenth century, Holland achieved supremacy as a seafaring nation and Dutchmen became preeminent in town planning. Within twenty years they founded five important towns overseas: Batavia (now Jakarta) in 1619, New Amsterdam (New York) in 1625, Mauritstad (now Recife, Brazil), Willemstad (Curaçao) in 1635, and Capetown (S. Africa) 1637. The Dutch were also called in to plan Mannheim (1606) and Gothenburg (1621).

The plan of Batavia is noteworthy (Plate 39), since it reflects the ideas of the theoretician Simon Stevin, who championed rational, modular layout based on standard house sizes and the linear extension of towns (Plate 40).

In England, the City of London experimented with colonization in Ulster. Twenty-three new town sites were designated.[29] The planning of these Irish new towns provided an important precedent for the later colonial ventures in America (see pp. 33–35).

On the continent some important towns were founded for Protestant refugees (Freudenstadt, Mannheim, Hanau, and Anspach). More importantly, the Scandinavian area became a theater of colonization. Following foundations of the Danes under Christian IV, the Swedish crown embarked on its own colonization program in the Baltic. From 1628 on Sweden possessed a competent surveying and fortification corps, and numerous towns could be started concurrently. Thus the number of Finnish towns doubled within seventeen years.[30]

During the eighteenth century the main effort of colonization lay in the Americas. In Europe town creation focused on princely residence-towns (see pp. 9–11). In Africa and in Asia the foundation of colonial towns reached its zenith in the nineteenth century. The most important group was in Algiers and Tunisia where the French created some six hundred new settlements between 1836 and 1914 using regular "castrum"-type plans.

In the British Dominions administrative centers were often based on carefully thought out, sensible plans, as in the case of Adelaide in 1837 (Plate 41). In their colonies the British largely contented themselves with building garden suburbs or "civil lines" next to the native towns; wherever they had to resort to comprehensive planning, formal grids were laid out (Port Said, 1865; Khartum, 1910), sometimes enlivened by decorative diagonal avenues.

Latecomers among colonizers, the Italians planned numerous settlements in Libya primarily to accommodate the twenty thousand Italian colonists sent from the home country during 1938–39. Their plans closely resemble the layout of the five Fascist new towns created in the Pontine marshes, which were initiated by Littoria in 1932.[31]

Nineteenth-century colonial planning did not contribute any new ideas to spatial organization but it did help spread the grid plan around the globe. By strengthening the urban network, it also prepared the base for the urbanization process that followed decolonization.

Hispanoamerican new towns: the Laws of the Indies

The Hispanic colonization of the Americas is the most impressive example in history of new town building guided by a uniform policy. From the start the foundation and layout of new towns was regulated by increasingly precise royal ordinances, later collected and codified by Philip II. This code of 1573 set the formal framework for an urbanization process which lasted three centuries with unbroken continuity.[32]

The Laws summarize the experience of half a century from the time that town building started in 1496 with the first permanent settlement in Santo Domingo.'

In Hispanoamerican practice—as before in Rome—the legal existence of the town had to be established by a foundation ritual before any construction could begin. A town plan was required before the foundation act could take place, and to assure the viability of the foundation a minimum number of settlers had to commit themselves to stay. The Laws offer advice on site selection and prescribe a pragmatic subdivision pattern: The plat, or *traza,* was to be a regular checkerboard, staked out with the help of a ruler and rope, starting from a central square.

Thirty *vecinos,* or freeholders, were required for a foundation: considering family size and servants, this implies a minimum of three hundred persons. The corresponding nine-square plan (Plate 42) of about 12 ha. consisted of a central public square and eight surrounding blocks. Each block was divided into four *solares* yielding a total of thirty-two lots, two of which were to be reserved for public buildings. The more ambitious "one hundred *vecino*" plan of Caracas (Plate 43) and of Mendoza (1562) (Plate 44a) consist of twenty-five squares. 7×7 and 9×9 square plats were also used during the seventeenth and the eighteenth centuries. Exceptionally large *trazas* were laid out if the town was destined to become a provincial capital, as in the case of Lima (1535—300 ha.; Plate 45) or Buenos Aires (1583—345 ha.; Plate 46).

The Laws are unusually farsighted in providing for the growth of the town area: sufficient open space is to be reserved "to permit the town to expand in accordance with the original layout." A belt of unbuilt land had to be reserved, of an area 3 to 4 times larger than the town plat.

Beyond this "green belt," farm lots were staked out for commoners (*peonerías*) and for noblemen (*caballerías*) (Plate 44b).[33] Great attention was lavished on the central square or *plaza mayor* which was to be the true heart of the new community. As a place of assembly it was destined to remain empty and, because of its size, the framing buildings remain subordinate, rather than dominating the space.[34] The location of the *plaza mayor* is in the center of the *traza* with the exception of port cities, where it is to face the waterfront. Although the Laws specify rectangular plazas—fit for tournaments—in practice they were mostly traced as perfect squares. American plazas are more regular and also larger then the contemporary squares in Europe. Since the need for visual enclosure of the vast plazas required the concentration of all substantial buildings along the edges, the plazas acquired a distinct civic center character—later reinforced by the removal of market functions to other parts of the city. The typical arrangement places the church and episcopal palace on the east side facing the town hall (*cabildo*); the North side is occupied by the royal houses (court, customs, mint, arsenal) and the south side by the palaces of the leading citizens.[35]

These plazas are still adequate as the centers of modern towns of up to a half-million inhabitants and even in large capital cities government functions remain anchored in their immediate vicinity: Plate 47 shows the outline of the original *traza* on an aerial photograph of Caracas. The modern government center is a few blocks south of the center of the colonial town.

A characteristic feature of Latin American foundations was the practice of assigning the corner lots of the *traza* to monasteries.[36] The ability to attract monastic institutions was the key to the success of a new foundation, very much like the need of modern shopping centers to assure the participation of two or more well-known department stores. The monasteries were social and educational centers, each dominating a small plaza which became the focus of life of their respective *barrio*.[37] As the town grew around the monasteries they became increasingly central to their *barrio*, which developed into the cellular unit of the Latin American town.

There has been much discussion about the spiritual origins of the Laws which Reps called "the most important documents in the history of urban development."[38] Stanislawski demonstrated [39] that the instructions concerning site selection had been copied from Aristotle, but otherwise he was wrong in overemphasizing the Renaissance and humanistic elements which represent late embellishments of the basic corpus.[40] Kubler is correct in pointing out that the greater part of the actual work of urbanization had been accomplished before 1573 when the statutes were first codified.[41]

The direct ancestry of the initial practice can be traced to the siege-town of Santa Fé de Granada (1492, Plate 48) and earlier agro-military towns of the peninsular reconquest based on medieval castrametation works.[42]

A most important factor, generally overlooked, was the shaping of the instructions by members of the monastic orders who dominated the colonial Council (*Concejo de Indias*) and whose thinking was influenced by theological speculation about the ideal Christian city. Such a concept is most precisely described by the Franciscan encyclopedist Eiximenis in a volume that first appeared in print in 1484.[43]

Eiximenis specifies a square town consisting of 64 blocks and of a size of 65 ha. which is sufficient to accomodate 10,000 people.[44] His town was to have a central plaza, surrounded by public buildings and a cathedral, and each of its four *barrios* was to have its monastery dominating a minor square. This plan has obvious similarities with the standard 5×5 and 7×7 square plat of the Latin American new towns with their monastic institutions in each quarter. Not only is such a disposition not mentioned in the Laws, but they also recommend long rectangular *plazas mayores* and emphasize that the main church, or *iglesia mayor,* should not be located there but in a quiet spot *off* the noise and animation of the plaza.

In spite of its medieval origins, the colonial pattern based on the Law of the Indies proved so convenient and efficient a tool that even after the breakup of the Spanish empire its successor states adhered to the spirit of the code in laying out further new towns.[45] The pattern persisted being used for nineteenth-century suburbs—and the tradition is still perpetuated by the *pobladores* of modern squatter settlements who often apply a regular checkerboard layout, as in the case of some of the Lima *barriadas.*[46]

North America: colonial towns and internal colonization

The beginnings of new town planning in North America lag a full century behind Latin America.

In New England, planned villages occurred around 1637 (Charleston, Cambridge, New Haven, Hartford, etc.) Simple orthogonal plans were drawn up to serve the needs of small homogeneous groups of 250 to 300 people.[47] A characteristic of these plans was the reservation of a central open space, the "commons"—eight acres in Hartford, sixteen acres in New Haven where it occupies one-ninth of the entire city area. The New Haven plan is a perfect square formed by three times three blocks resembling the standard Hispanoamerican plan for "thirty *vecinos,*" except for the fact that the New Haven blocks are unusually large (825 ft. square compared to 450 or 300 ft. in Latin America).

Early attempts at new town legislation were made both in Virginia (1662) and in Maryland (1683). A number of town sites of fifty and one hundred acres respectively were designated. Grid plans were drawn to accommodate one hundred to two hundred families on half-acre lots. These modest attempts to regularize town building encountered much resistance and had little impact.[48]

The building of Philadelphia was the first implementation on American soil of a plan concept with a scope comparable to the contemporary European new towns. The famous plan of 1683 prepared by Thomas Holme—William Penn's surveyor—stretches a grid of fifty-foot-wide streets over an area of two square miles (512 ha.). It is divided in four quarters by the cross of two one hundred-foot-wide avenues with a ten-acre central square and one eight-acre square in the middle of each quadrant.[49] Assuming that the original intent was to build homes on one-half-acre lots, this would have implied populations of 3,000 to 5,000 persons in each quadrant served by a neighborhood park (Plate 49). The growth of Philadelphia has been rapid. The town profited from the great fire and following plague of London which frightened some prosperous people into moving to Penn's "green country town that will never burn."

Of the numerous towns founded in New France the little fort of Detroit (1701) has the simplicity of a medieval bastide, while plans for Mobile (1711) and New Orleans (1722) resemble Hispanoamerican models. The plan of Mobile is an elongated rectangle formed by 5×10 blocks with a Place d'Armes separated from the river by a fort. The similarity with the sixteenth-century plan of Buenos Aires (Plate 46) is unmistakable.

In the eighteenth century the prize for innovative planning in America must be awarded to Savannah, Ga. Planned around 1733 by James Oglethorpe, the basic cellular unit is no more the block, but a ward consisting of forty-eight lots grouped around public open space. On two sides of the square, eight lots were reserved for public buildings. (Plate 50). The orderly expansion of the town could take place through the multiplication of these little neighborhoods, each serving about four hundred people.[50] This remarkable concept was followed in practice for the next one hundred twenty years. Common land was reserved from the beginning to permit this extension, and beyond this land-reserve the orthogonal pattern was pushed into the country, providing for five-acre garden lots and forty-four-acre farms within an overall road-grid of one mile square.

This idea of orthogonal division of country land reoccurs on tremendous scale in 1785 with the Land Ordinance of the Continental Congress regarding the Northwest Territories. The system consists of six mile square townships each divided into thirty-six sections of one mile square, similar to the Roman *centuriatio* (Plate 50a).

The adoption of this supergrid for the survey and disposal of western lands effectively stretched the checkerboard pattern across the continent. Later federal legislation established half-section town sites of 320 acres, and the rectangular town limits strongly implied further town division by the use of a grid plan which became the trade mark of American towns during the nineteenth century. Few indeed are the deviations from this pattern, whether planned by religious groups, railroad companies, or for industry.

In California, where the Mexican government carried out town planning according to the Laws of the Indies until 1835 (Sonoma), the two traditions finally merged. General Vallejo, the Mexican officer who planned Sonoma, cheerfully carried on platting the American cities of Vallejo and Benicia.

Russia: internal colonization

6 Plan of Tobolsk, Siberia, rendering second half seventeenth century.

The Russian advance toward Siberia began in the sixteenth century—with the foundation of a first Russian colony in Tobolsk, 1587 (Fig. 6).

The construction of the Trans-Siberian Railroad during 1892–1905 marks the beginning of the systematic colonization of the Asian half of the Russian empire. The mass migration that followed reached proportions comparable to the earlier westward wave of pioneers in the United States. Important new towns like Novosibirsk (1893) (then Novonikolayevsk) were built along the railway line; earlier foundations like Khabarovsk (1858) and Vladivostok (1880) boomed.

After the revolution, large-scale agricultural development became possible by the forced resettlement of the expropriated kulaks after 1929. New towns were also founded by members of the Communist youth movement, like Komsomolsk on the Amur (1932). During the second World War the relocation of vital industries resulted in a series of new towns beyond the Urals. Internal colonization by the creation of new towns is still official Soviet doctrine. Continued resettlement is considered imperative "to equalize the economic development in different parts of the country." [51] Since the goal is to ensure adequate amenities with the lowest expenditures, the optimum size will obviously vary with the climate, topography, and other local conditions. Towns of optimum size constitute the basis for future resettlement. Taking into account both construction and operating costs, Soviet planners advocate town sizes between 100,000 and 300,000 inhabitants. The threshold of 100,000 is considered to be the minimum to sustain an adequate level and variety of cultural and welfare activities.

The new towns are planned by central planning institutions and financed by the state. Rapid town building is assured by rigid adherence of planning norms, the use of standardized building designs and the application on a large-scale of prefabricated elements in construction. The basic building block of Soviet urbanism is the prefabricated apartment building six stories high and housing 500 to 1,000 persons. Four to fifteen large buildings form a superblock, or *kvartal,* grouping 3,600 to 7,500 people on an area of 9 to 15 hectares, with an average net density of 400 to 500 people per hectare, twice as high as in British new towns. Establishments of daily use are located within a radius of 300 to 400 m. from the buildings. (A *kvartal* would be equipped with an eight-year school, kindergarten, dining hall, grocery, repair shops, and athletic fields). Two of four kvartals form a *microrayon* or neighborhood with 10,000 to 15,000 people in an area of 30 to 50 hectares with a gross density of 300 people per ha. The *microrayon* groups establishments of periodic use within a radius of about one km. This includes clubs, cinemas, department stores and food markets, bank, post office, polyclinic and health centers, gymnasium, etc. The essential idea of the *microrayon* is the same as that of the western neighborhood: it is a living unit based on the "catchment area" of local educational, shopping and other services. Since the *microrayon* is the basic cellular component of Soviet community, its spatial organization varies little with the size of the towns.

The high densities of the Soviet *kvartal* permit easy access to bus or subway stations; by contrast little provision is made for parking space for automobiles. Time will tell whether the Russians will be able to restrict the number of private automobiles by car-hire schemes and taxi pools in addition to good public transit. The experience of the British and Scandinavian new towns shows that increased car ownership can raise havoc with well-meant plans and expensive modifications become necessary, particularly in the center areas. The main defect of Soviet new towns is their drabness and monotony, which result from the standardized planning design and construction methods generally applied.

In quantitative terms, the Soviet new towns have been a tremendous success: In 1959 the Soviet Union (not including the territories acquired during the war) could boast of 1,672 towns; of these 670 were built after 1926 and no less then 200 represent completely new towns containing today well over four million people.[52]

New towns of Israel

Israel is the only other modern state to employ internal colonization as a fundamental concept of national development. The policy was launched when it was recognized that the uneven distribution of the population between the coastal strip and the inland districts was a threat to the security of the state.

In rural areas the population was predominantly Arab: the small Jewish settlements were either cooperative moshavim or communistic *kibbutzim* with a social organization which excluded their enlargement into medium-size towns. In fact, in 1948 the Jewish population was concentrated in the three cities of Tel Aviv, Jerusalem, and Jaffa. Yet the new town policy was not a decongestion measure, but relied for its success on immigration. Although economic considerations did not predominate, it was nevertheless hoped that the new towns would serve as centers for the rural areas. This assumption proved erroneous since the small country of Israel with its good communication system forms a single market.

The National Planning Office constituted in 1948 has been responsible for the planning of new towns. In a first phase between 1948–51, eighteen new towns were founded. Ten of these were based on Arab towns abandoned by their original population. Of these, Beer Sheba (Plates 52, 53) developed into the supply center of the Negev with a population of 100,000 people, and Ashkelon on the Mediterranean coast grew due to its resort appeal. The growth of the other towns has been disappointing. From 1952 to 1957 ten more new towns were added, among them the port cities of Elath and Ashdod. Ashdod is planned for an initial population of 150,000 and should eventually become one of the largest ports in the eastern Mediterranean. Since 1960 only two new strategic settlements, recruited exclusively of Israel-born *sabra* youth, have been started: Karmiel (Plate 54) and Arad, each planned for a target population of 40 to 50,000 people.

The town plans of the first phase derived their inspiration from the British garden city movement. Their low-density sprawl has been criticized for wasting valuable land, for high cost of development and maintenance of their infrastructure, and lack of urbanity. Since 1958 greater densities and higher buildings are preferred: an example of this trend is the model neighborhood in Beer Sheba consisting of three- to four-story blocks and "carpet" type patio houses, with an overall net density of 260 persons per ha.

The widespread use of large-scale prefabricated elements makes most Israeli towns monotonous. However in Karmiel and Arad, attempts are made to develop an urban design vocabulary appropriate to Israel's climate.

To maintain a steady growth rate of the new towns, it has been hoped that 25 percent of the newly arrived immigrants will settle in them. Since 1958 large numbers of Sephardic Jews from North Africa and the Middle East have been assigned to the new towns, but this segregation and the fact that lack of jobs resulted in unemployment gave a bad name to some of the new towns and tended to discredit the entire program. Of the thirty new towns only four or five have proved economically viable, and the others still require subsidies for their continued existence. Due to their slow initial growth, they have never achieved critical mass and the momentum needed to become self-supporting.

It is now generally admitted that the creation of fewer but larger new towns would have made more sense economically. Yet, in terms of its original goals, the program has been a success. The combined population of the new towns grew by 1961 to 276,000, passed 400,000 in 1964, and presently accounts for 16 percent of the total population of Israel.

4 INDUSTRIAL TOWNS

Definitions　　New industrial towns are planned to exploit location-bound natural resources or to provide growth poles for a regional development policy. The town itself is created to accommodate the necessary labor force, and its site is chosen as a function of conflicting needs to maximize accessibility and at the same time to avoid the noise, pollution, and traffic generated by industry.

As a rule, development goals and the objective of efficient production receive priority over welfare considerations, which at best are admitted to be instrumental in the attainment of the primary objectives.[1] Thus, at least at the start, directly productive investment (in industry, roads, etc.) will be favored over social cost type investment (housing, schools, etc.). This policy is in marked contrast to the investment schedule of new towns created to decongest metropolitan areas. Such towns also offer industrial employment: yet their planning is not custom-tailored to the needs of a specific industrial employer, but relies on an attractive living environment to entice industries to relocate or to invest in the new town. Accordingly, in industrial towns jobs are provided at a faster rate than housing and social amenities, while in the decongestion-type new towns employment often lags behind the number of resident job-seekers. This may result in commuting to the industrial town from considerable distances,[2] while the decongestion new towns are more likely to have a large percentage of out-commuters.

The need for the creation of new industrial towns arises in the transition period from a preindustrial to an industrial society. In times of intensive or forced industrialization the percentage of those employed in manufacturing will rise above 30 percent of the total labor force and the creation of adequate housing for industrial workers becomes a pressing problem. In countries with a dense urban network, new industry can draw on the population and services offered by existing towns. In Western Europe—apart from some nineteenth-century experimentation—the creation of new industrial towns has been an exception.[3]

The Soviet Union pioneered in building new industrial towns as instruments of internal colonization. Following the Russian example, new industrial towns have also been built by the Communist regimes in postwar Eastern Europe. More recently, developing countries like India, Venezuela, Iran, and Turkey embarked on a vigorous industrialization policy making use of the creation of new towns.

There are obvious advantages in locating the new towns close to the source of raw materials but this may impose the selection of a site in harsh and inhospitable climates.

Kitimat [4] (Canada) is exposed to incessant rain, snow, and winds; Vorkuta (USSR) on the 65th parallel north is built on permafrost ground; in Ariashahr (Iran) summer temperatures exceed 42° centigrade. The microclimate of such sites can be improved: in Dushanbe (Tadjikistan, USSR) the planting of forests and the creation of lakes helped to reduce the oppressive heat by 4–5° centigrade.

Good communications are even more important to heavy industry than proximity to fixed resources. The site of Gary, Indiana (Plate 59) was selected by the United States Steel Company because it was halfway between the iron ore of Minnesota and the coal of Pennsylvania and at the same time had a convenient outlet to the Great Lakes via the Calumet River. Shipments of bulk goods (ore, limestone, coal) to the plant, as well as the distribution of finished or semifinished products, make access to a seaport, canal, or a navigable river highly desirable. The steel towns of Nova Huta (Poland), Dunaujvaros (Hungary), and Ciudad Guyana (Venezuela) depend on river transport and the Volkswagen town of Wolfsburg (Germany), on a canal, for their bulk shipments.

The major town-forming types of industry are iron and steel mills (Gary, Rourkela, Ariashahr, Ciudad Guyana, etc.), aluminum smelting (Kitimat, Sabned [Guinea]), heavy machine building and armament works (Salzgitter, Magnitogorsk, Volgograd), petrochemical works (El Tablazo [Venezuela], Aliaga, [Turkey]) and automobile plants (Wolfsburg, [Germany], Togliatti, [USSR]).

During the nineteenth century many company towns were created by private enterprise. Due to their monostructured economic base such towns proved very vulnerable to market fluctuations and depressions. It is now generally admitted that private industry is not the ideal agent for the development and continued management of a new town, and even in market economies some government participation is welcome.

The simple economic structure of industrial towns makes it possible to predict accurately future population levels from the planned employment in the basic industry.[5] Thus the provision of housing and of institutions can be coordinated with stages of industrial development.

In developing countries the use of simple "multipliers" in predicting future population is much less reliable. Since migrants arrive at random and proceed to construct their shelter, the growth rate cannot be directly related to job provision schedules. Because the margin of error in predicting may be considerable, the pilot plans must be more flexible than in developed countries.

The recruitment of population poses a problem, particularly in remote areas with extreme climates. In developing countries the building of a new town is more likely to trigger off spontaneous migration but it is difficult to attract the skilled workers, technicians, and administrative staff. Antagonism develops easily between construction workers and the skilled workers employed in the town-forming industry if this second group is favored in the allocation of housing and amenities.

At least initially, industrial towns suffer from a lack of female employment, which leads to an unbalanced sex ratio with men far outnumbering women. To achieve equilibrium, labor-intensive light industry must be provided. In market economies this is difficult to achieve since the secondary industries would have to offer wages and fringe benefits on a comparable level with the basic industry and are thus priced out of the market.

Unless the town offers a pleasant living environment, the industry will suffer from a high turnover of key personnel. Since a stable work force is essential for the efficient operation of industry, the quality of the physical environment must be recognized as an important factor for successful development. The layout of industrial towns is determined largely by the desire to minimize the journey to work. This is of paramount importance in industrial towns where employment is often concentrated in a single area. Even if different industries are proposed, "linkages," economies of scale and of proximity may dictate their clustering.

In nineteenth-century industrial towns (Saltaire, Lowell) the workers housing was often placed directly across from the factory gates. Later plans separated the town from the industry by a canal (Wolfsburg) or by a green buffer zone of 1–2 km. (Dunaujvaros, Plate 61b). At present a separation of 10–15 km. between residential areas and heavy industry is the accepted practice (Ciudad Guyana, Ariashahr, El Tablazo).

Such long distances presuppose efficient public transit: in Wolfsburg plant-owned buses supplement the municipal bus system. In many cases the linear relationship between the industry and the urban center would justify the use of a rail shuttle service as in Wuppertal, yet to my knowledge no new industrial town can boast of this type of equipment.

Historical survey   Just as the colonial city owes its origins to the military camp and the art of "castrametation," the ancestry of the planned industrial town can be traced back to the labor camp. In preindustrial societies the only large-scale organized labor force was employed in the construction industry. Division of labor, specialization, complexity, and size led to a highly efficient organization of production which Mumford describes as a "human machine." It was to provide housing for such a labor force that the first planned workers' settlements were built in Pharaonic Egypt at Hotep Sesostris (Plate 55) (now Kahun, 1890 B.C.) and Akhetaten (now El Amarna, 1360 B.C.)[6] A minimum adequate standard for housing workmen and their families was established: single and double rows of identical houses, none too different from the nineteenth-century workers' "terraces" in England.

Prior to the industrial revolution most manufacturing was carried out in small workshops. Eventually, the need for naval yards, arsenals, and gun foundries led to fairly large-scale industrial enterprises. In fifteenth-century Venice, a regular production line for outfitting galleys was introduced. A large permanent work force eventually compelled the city council to build *domus communis*—municipal housing—for the workers of the naval yard—*per merito e non per amore Dei* (1530).[7] Apart from such exceptions, the provision of public housing was long confined to almshouses. This association with charity and paternalism made the acceptance of industry-provided housing long unpalatable.

Two planned industrial towns of the eighteenth century are worth mentioning: the factory-fortress of Jekaterinburg in Russia, built in 1730 (gun foundries) and the salt-works at Chaux, designed by the French architect Ledoux in the 1770s. Both plans placed the production sheds in the middle, surrounded by the workers' housing: a disposition which severely restricts the possibility of plant expansion.

At the time of these mercantilists and Baroque experiments on the continent, England was already affected by the industrial revolution. Unprecedented crowding and deprivation soon led to epidemics and riots. Paternalistic concern with the workers' living conditions and morality, and the desire to remove them from big-city agitation brought forth the Utopian Socialist movement with its proposals for model industrial villages. Marx and Engels were to denounce these attempts for increasing the workers' dependence on his employer but the fact remains that the movement pioneered with many valid social welfare ideas on which even Marx and Engels drew.

As of 1816, Robert Owen, in Scotland, championed the creation of new communities to combine work with study and leisure and established 1,200 persons as the minimum threshold. In 1832, the Frenchman, Charles Fourier, launched the idea of the *Phalanstère,* proposing self-contained communities for 1,620 persons, based on the notion that on any given day 810 distinct characters were needed to maintain essential production and services. Both industry and the community were to be housed in a "social palace"—a single megastructure 3600 feet long.[8]

Owen's ideas influenced the American, Robert Lowell, who conceived the prototype of the New England mill town. The mills were to be placed between a river and a parallel canal, with employee housing between the canal and a major road, along which public buildings, shops, and private residences would be located. These principles were first tested in 1822 in a new town on the Merrimac river named after Lowell. As an innovation, dormitory housing was provided for the female workers, high moral standards being assured by stern housemothers. New England mill towns enjoyed a thirty-year boom period: in ten years the population of Lowell reached 11,000 persons.[9]

In contemporary England, James Silk Buckingham called for the creation of new towns with populations of 10,000 each as a "blueprint for full employment by mass production" (Plate 56). However, actual accomplishments remained modest in size and in impact.

In 1850 Titus Salt built Saltaire as a "self-sufficient industrial community" of 4,536 persons. In Akroydon, Colonel Akroyd hoped to uplift his workers morality by "a positive aesthetic environment" to assure "more durable social values." [10]

In France, Jean Baptiste Godin carried out Fourier's idea of the *palais social* by housing all workers of his foundry at Guise in a single communal building (Plate 57). Alas, the workers objected to strict regimentation and the paternalistic experiment misfired—as it did two decades later in Pullman, Illinois.

Pullman was built in 1880 as a model town for the workers of the railroad carriage factory (Plate 58). Planned on a 1600 hectare area, the town was unusual for its numerous public buildings. In eleven years the population grew to 8,000. However, the workers resented their bondage of depending on Pullman both for their jobs and their housing and in a famous strike (1894) forced the company to divest itself of the town. This precedent warned other American companies to avoid investment in imaginative planning. The unrelieved monotony of the grid plan of Gary (1905) exemplifies the resulting minimalist tendency (Plate 59).

The turn of the century was marked by two remarkable proposals: the first, Ebenezer Howard's call for garden cities is discussed in chapter 5. The second was Tony Garnier's project of a *Cité Industrielle* for 35,000 people—incidentally the same size as Howard's garden cities (Fig. 7).[11]

Garnier's ideal town was based on metallurgical industry and was to receive clean energy from its hydroelectric plant. The town forms a band six km. long and 600 m. wide with an interurban electric trolley in its middle. Industry occupies 50 percent of the developed area in a separate zone at one end of the site. Garnier's project anticipates many ideas later propagated by CIAM and Le Corbusier, such as the "functional city," minimum adequate housing, and the "factory in the green." [12]

Around 1920, Le Corbusier put forward the idea of a strictly zoned separation of urban functions, separation of vehicular and pedestrian movement and—in defiance of Howard's garden city concept—"super-densities" of 1,000 persons per hectare and above.[13] Some of these theories were first put to test in the Soviet Union, where the revolution had created unprecedented conditions for innovation and experiments in urban planning.

7 Diagram of the *Cité Industrielle* by Tony Garnier, 1904.

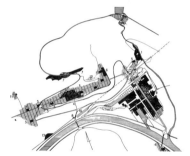

1 Old town
2 Railroad station
3 Residential areas
4 Town center
5 Primary schools
6 Professional schools
7 Hospitals
8 Town railroad station
9 Industry
10 Railroad yard
11 Cemetery
12 Public park with old castle
13 Slaughter houses

The Soviet experience and Eastern Europe

The first five-year plan (1928–32) was the heroic time of Soviet town planning: sixty new cities were founded mostly in areas where the settlement network was scarce; among the most important were:

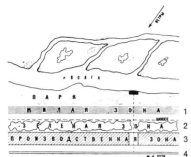

8 Diagram of a linear city (Stalingrad) by N. A. Miliutin, 1930.

Karaganda, in the Kazakh coal basin, already started in 1926.

Magnitogorsk, in the Urals, planned in 1929 (a competition).

Zaporozhe, in the Ukraine, founded in 1930 in connection with the Dneprostroi hydroelectric works.

Stalingrad, on the Volga, built up in 1929–30.

Numerous architect-planners labored to put the theories of "constructivism" and "disurbanization" of the architect, T. Khasin, into practice. N. A. Miliutin, in his famous treatise about the problem of building the socialist city, or *Sotsgorod,* propagated the idea of the linear plan. His linear industrial city was to be a plan as efficient as a factory assembly line and one that would break down the distinction between urban and rural proletariat (Fig. 8). Also, Soviet modernists considered that a linear plan would form "an artery along which the principles of Karl Marx can be pumped." [14]

Miliutin's basic scheme consisted of six parallel zones: a railway zone (4); the industrial zone (3); a green zone no less than 500 m. wide with a main arterial highway passing through it (2); the residential zone (1); and the recreation zone with agricultural fields beyond—or, in the case of Stalingrad, across the Volga River.

The plan of Magnitogorsk, as proposed by the OSA group (decentralists) was a ribbon some 30 km. long uniting the industrial center with collective farms. The commission was given, however, to a German "brigade" headed by Ernst May recently arrived from Frankfurt. His typical German Siedlung plan was modified after he left the USSR in the early 1930s.

The plan of Stalingrad, as initially proposed during the first five-year plan, stretched many kilometers along the Volga; the town was planned to be divided into five settlements, each with a population of 75,000–90,000 persons. Instead of individual houses there were to be "living combines." Eating, studying, and recreation were to take place in communal dining halls, study halls, gymnasiums—not unlike a university campus. To free women from housekeeping, children were to be raised communally. Most of these ideas were condemned as impractical already in the 1931 party plenum of the All-Union Communist Party and were soon abandoned.

Stalingrad was actually built around five industrial combines—a plan that had many defects: residential areas were cut off from the river by railway yards and industry and the gridiron layouts were imposed on the land regardless of topographic features. The siege of 1943 virtually destroyed this town, however, and the new plan cleared the waterfront and developed the entire riverfront as parks.

New town building continued during World War II. Between 1942 and 1944, sixty-seven new towns were built. These were of three different types:

1 Mining communities like Vorkuta in the Pechora mining basin, near the Arctic Circle;

2 Small settlements in the Urals expanded to form new towns;

3 New towns around railway stations where trains evacuating plants from the threatened western territories could unload.

The building of new industrial towns acquired new vigor after the war, particularly in the Asiatic areas of the USSR. According to B. Malisz, in 1959 out of a total of 1,672 towns in the USSR (not including territory acquired during the war) no less then 670 are of post-1926 vintage. Most of these are industrial towns.

Industrialization was, of course, not the only town-creating factor: satellite towns were also built (See pp. 66–67).

Now, about forty years after their foundation, some of the new towns have grown to impressive size: Karaganda, which in 1926 had a population of 116 persons, grew to 163,937 by 1939 and to 460,000 by 1972. Magnitogorsk and Novosibirsk passed a half-million inhabitants.

The creation of new industrial towns is still considered imperative for the location of efficient production. A population of 100,000 to 250,000 people is proposed as the optimum size for industrial towns, depending on local conditions and the goal of ensuring optimum amenities with the lowest expenditure.

Blokhine says that the size of 100,000 to 250,000 people "will sustain main branches of industry, yet the commuter problem can be controlled without great cost or time loss." [15] Nevertheless, economic criteria remain paramount: "The city general plan must ensure the highest possible increase in production per ruble of investment to reduce the amortization period of such an investment and to achieve good amenities with minimum construction and operating expenses." The planning of residential areas follows the fundamental concepts of the microrayon (See p. 36 and Plate 60).

During the decade following World War II, the People's Republics of Poland, Hungary, Czechoslovakia, and East Germany hastened to follow the example of the USSR in the creation of new "socialist towns." [16] Given the denser urban network in these countries, there was scant economic justification for the effort. Political motives predominated—to spread an industrial proletariat among the conservative peasants or in the case of Nova Huta near Cracow—to create a "socialist" counterpole to the fortress of nationlist traditions.

Being too close to Cracow (10 km.) Nova Huta never developed into a fully independent entity. Nova Tychy at 20 km. from Katowice became a dormitory satellite. Poor judgment in the choice of location made other towns very expensive: Dunaujvaros (Hungary) was placed above the Danube on a steep embankment which soon required costly consolidation works to prevent landslides (Fig. 9; Plates 61a, b).

The plans and buildings of this period were characterized by heavy-handed monumentalism. Their growth was hampered by various blunders: uneven investment flow; poor staging; housing provision that fell behind the creation of em-

9 Schematic plan of Dunaujvaros, Hungary.

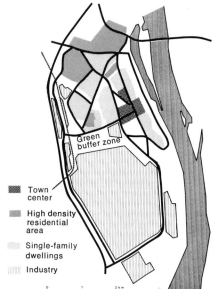

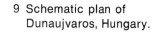

Green buffer zone

Town center

High density residential area

Single-family dwellings

Industry

0   1   2 km

ployment; and the creation of amenities and institutions that lagged behind the needs of the population.

Nevertheless, the new towns provided valuable planning experience and several have reached a viable size: Nova Huta has 150,000 inhabitants, Dunaujvaros 50,000. The eight new towns of Hungary account for 2 percent of the country's population.

Official disappointment with the new towns resulted in a change of policy: present efforts are directed toward "expanded towns" by the gradual restructuring of existing settlements, starting with the creation of a full-scale modern center, as in Salgotarján, Hungary (Plate 62).

It is interesting to compare the East European experiences with the development of Salzgitter and of Wolfsburg, two planned industrial towns founded shortly before the war in Germany.

Germany   **Salzgitter** Salzgitter, 25 km. South of Brunswick, owes its existence to the creation of the Hermann Göring armament works located in the vicinity of rich iron ore deposits. The plan, prepared by H. Rimpl in 1939, proposed a first stage population of 130,000 and a target size of 200,000 on a site of 1,925 ha.[17] The town was to have an oval shape circled by a rail rapid transit ring. The north-south axis was to connect the railroad station with the highway leading to the mines in the south; a monumental mall would lead from the central town square to the gates of the armament works, with two other avenues radiating to entrances of the Berlin-Hanover Autobahn.

The ordering principles of the plan seem to be derived from the Roman castrum with its street cross and forum. However, the town was to have a high ratio of public parks (20 percent) and private gardens (39 percent) with a low overall density of sixty-seven persons per ha. The National Socialist ideology professed a nearly mythical attachment to the German soil. The Reichscomissar für Siedlungswesen called on planners to reestablish the "Erdverbundenheit mit der Deutschen Muttererde," wherefrom came the postulate of providing each new dwelling unit with a garden. Such environments would presumably produce healthier human breeding stock in contrast to the crowded cities which suck out (*auslaugen*) the vitality of the folk-community. The ideological trend toward some form of agro-industrial urbanism was strengthened by the sensible demand to avoid crowding in industrial centers which might become targets for aerial bombardment. The internal organization of the towns was to reflect the structure of the party:

Group: 8–15 households; Block: 4 groups; Cell: 4–18 blocks; Sector (*Ortsgruppe*): 3–10 cells; Circle (*Kreis*): a number of sectors, up to 10,000 DUs or 50–60,000 people.[18]

Wolfsburg The town of Wolfsburg, 25 km. north of Brunswick, was created in 1938 to accommodate the workers of the Volkswagen works (Plate 63). The site was selected for its good east-west communications, the principal axis of goods movement in prewar Germany. An area of 3,000 ha. was acquired in 1938, and enlarged to 3,500 ha. in 1960.[19] The original plan of 1938, by P. Koller, placed the industry to the north of the canal, and grouped residential areas mainly between the canal and a hill to the south. The top of the hill was to be crowned by a group of representative buildings, forming an acropolis. This plan envisioned a population of 90,000 people. A new master plan was prepared in 1957 and updated in 1962 for a target population of 130,000. The 1972 land use map (Plate 64) is the most up-to-date adjusted version of the 1962 plan. In 1970 the town offered 78,000 jobs, attracting 34,057 commuters from the outside and the population approached 100,000 (Plate 65).

The environmental assets of Wolfsburg are unique for an industrial town: no dwelling is more than ten minutes walk from a large park, a lake, or a forest. Forty-one percent of the total city area is devoted to green areas. The industry occupies only twenty-two percent of the land (725 ha.), and the efficient road network requires only 7.6 percent. Car ownership is twice as high as the national average—one car for three persons—yet traffic flows smoothly on urban expressways. An efficient and well-used public bus system and a fleet of plant-owned buses reduce the peak loads. In the newer residential sectors pedestrian-vehicular separation is complete.

New Districts like Detmerode (Plate 65a) and Westhagen group 15,000 people each with gross densities of 128 persons per ha. High rise buildings are concentrated on the edges with flat, "carpet," or patio-type buildings, and a shopping center in the middle.

In Westhagen continuous bands of buildings define pedestrian corridors with a well-modulated spatial sequence (Plate 65b). Housing is not segregated by income and all districts are composed of two-thirds blue collar and one-third white collar residents.[20]

Wolfburg can boast of several examples of innovative architecture, such as Alvar Aalto's cultural center and church, Hans Scharoun's theater. The town offers excellent cultural productions and has acquired a regional role in culture, education, and health service (Plate 65c).[21] The present layout of Wolfsburg has lost the monumental pretensions of the Koller plan—it is informal and makes excellent use of the existing landscape. The town could be considered as a model for industrial towns were it not for its overdependence on a single employer. Sixty-eight percent of the total employed labor force in Wolfsburg works for Volkswagen. There is little employment for women, who fill only ten percent of all jobs.

Wolfsburg demonstrates the strength, but also the weakness, of an industrial town in a market economy. The dynamic Volkswagen plant is the source of the riches of the town and sponsors some of its unique amenities and equipment; on the other hand the prosperity of the town is totally dependent on a single enterprise and thus on fluctuations of the demand in international markets.

Developing countries

The creation of new industrial towns is vital for those developing countries just entering the transitional phase toward an industrial society. Impressed by the success of the Soviet Union with forced industrialization, numerous Third World nations are experimenting with five-year plans.

The new industrial towns also serve as regional growth poles, helping to deflect migration and easing the demographic pressure on the capital and other large cities with insufficient job-potential and chronic underemployment. Since 1950 the Indian government had emphasized the creation of new towns based on heavy industry. Vast iron and steel-works have been built with the help of Russian, American, and German aid, such as Bhilai (24 km. from Nagpur), Durgapur (188 km. northeast of Calcutta), or Rourkela (415 km. west of Calcutta [Orissa State]). Each plant will support a new town with a population of 100,000 to 125,000 people.

The most interesting plan is that of Rourkela, designed by the German planner, Konrad Seiler. The steel works built by Krupp and Demag will employ 14,000 workers and support a population of 100,000. Industry is separated from the town by a low range of hills at a distance of only 5 km., which permits the steelworkers to commute by bicycle. The town will consist of twenty "villages," each with 5,000 people. A major collector road running through a continuous green strip connects the town with its industries. The town area is 1,500 ha. (without industry) and gross densities will be around 60 persons per ha (Fig. 10).

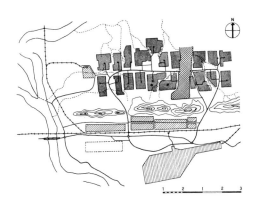

10 Plan of Rourkela, India. New industrial town, based on steel mill works.

The towns of Ciudad Guayana, Venezuela and Ariashahr, Iran invite comparison since both are based on nationally owned steel mills of similar output. Both are being built by semi-autonomous state development corporations and while the planning of Ciudad Guayana profited from advice by North American experts, the Iranian town was planned by the Soviet State Town Planning Institute, GIPROGOR, in Moscow.

The Site of Ciudad Guayana is at the confluence of the Caroní river with the navigable Orinoco, 500 km. from Caracas. Nearby, the Guri dam assures cheap electric energy, and there are vast reserves of iron ore in the vicinity. The town has the potential to become the center not only of Venezuelan Guayana but also of the oil-rich eastern region north of the Caroní.

Ariashahr Ariashahr is located some 40 km. from Isfahan—the second largest city of Iran—on a plateau characterized by extreme temperatures.[22] The town is 15 km. distant from the industry and is protected from pollution by a range of hills.[23] The Master Plan—approved in 1968—predicts a town population of 300,000 persons. Although the overall density is 100 persons per ha., the town structure is compact: municipal buildings, a hotel, and a mosque form a dominating group atop a 170-m.-high hill from which the town's major avenue descends in a spiral. Along this spine are ranged the residential sectors, each accommodating 25,000 to 30,000 inhabitants. This arrangement is reminiscent of a theoretical scheme published in 1962 by G. A. Gradow (Fig. 11), which grouped six residential sectors in a U-shape around a focal town center. One-third of the population is assigned housing in four- to nine-story high apartment buildings, 17 percent is to be housed in two story, and the rest in single story blocks.

Dwelling sizes are graduated for four occupational classes. For an unskilled worker 12 sq. m. of living space is proposed and about twice as much for top administrative personnel. As it rigidly follows Russian standards, the plan makes no provision for reception areas for squatters. Although the new town is bound to attract disorderly migration, no mention is made anywhere of unemployed or underemployed groups. It is assumed that the ratio of employed total population will be 33 percent, which is optimistic considering that it is 18 percent in other industrial towns in Iran.[24]

Ciudad Guayana As Ariashahr was built *ex nihilo,* the planning of the town and of the steel mill could be coordinated. In Ciudad Guayana the steel mill was built before any plan for a new town had emerged (Plate 66). In 1960—when the development corporation CVG[25] was created—already 30,000 people lived within the designated area of the new town. The bulk of this population was concentrated on the

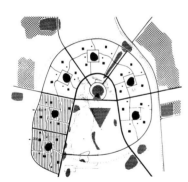

11 Schematic plan of a town of 240,000 persons by G. A. Gradow.

east side of the Caroní River in the town of San Felix, 25 km. from the industry. The little company town of Porto Ordaz was on the west side of the river but still 15 km. distant from the steel mill.

In 1961 the CVG turned to the Massachusetts Institute of Technology and to Harvard University for planning assistance.[26] By that time, the influx of unskilled immigrants, at a monthly rate of 1,000 persons, imposed ad hoc decisions before a plan concept could crystallize. The Venezuelan *Plan de la Nación* of 1962 set ambitious targets for the development of Guayana: ten percent of all public or private investment was to be funneled to projects in the region, including the vast Guri dam, 90 km. from the new town (Plate 67). Optimistic projections by the economists first fixed the 1980 population of Ciudad Guayana at 650,000 people.[27] These figures, soon revised to 450,000 and then to 300,000, affected the physical plan and development strategy.[28]

Urban form was greatly influenced by the decision to concentrate all heavy industry in proximity to the steel mill. A linear structure was proposed to link the industries with the existing nodes of settlement by bridging the Caroní River (Plates 68a, b). Along this spine, the logical location of the center would have been the geographically prominent peninsula that forms the bridgehead of the new crossing. Growth between this center and the existing towns could have resulted in a single city mass. Compact urban form, with higher densities along the spine, would have saved on infrastructure investment and operating cost of a public transit system (Plate 69). However, the CVG favored a low-density pattern and computer tests based on an accessibility model indicated an alternate site for the center: closer to the industry. This new site, Alta Vista, had the disadvantage of being far removed from the rivers which are the major environmental asset of the town; it was also isolated from then existing development (Plate 70). The decision of the CVG to develop Alta Vista as the town center was coupled with a "two-city strategy," grouping two-thirds of the future population on the west side and relegating San Felix to a satellite position (Figs. 12a, b). The inherent dichotomy of the town, split by the river, was thus reinforced: unskilled and low income families on the east side; steel workers and employees to the west.[29]

The preference of immigrants for San Felix as a center of animation (Plate 71) resulted in its rapid growth, forcing a revision of the strategic plan, which now allocates half of the population to each side of the town, leaving Alta Vista in an excentric position.[30] In addition to this liability, private business shrank from the risk of locating on isolated Alta Vista and preferred investment in nearby Porto Ordaz.[31] Except for a CVG building, Alta Vista remains undeveloped, while the continuing boom of Porto Ordaz threatens to perpetuate the little company town as the center of Ciudad Guayana (Plate 72). This experience focuses attention on

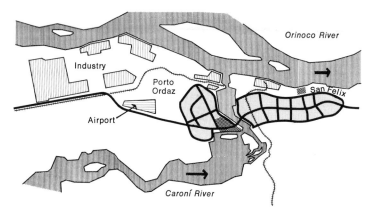

12 a. Ciudad Guayana, diagram of single-city strategy.

12 b. Ciudad Guayana, diagram of two-cities strategy.

psychological factors in locational choice and discredits overreliance on mechanistic models based on the selection of easily quantifiable criteria. It also demonstrates that in new towns built around existing settlements the primacy of a new center can only be asserted by the immediate provision of prestige facilities that definitely overshadow the attractions of the old center. Given a free choice, new investment will strengthen the existing center and put the new center at increasing disadvantage.[32]

Alta Vista may still become viable once the town has grown to a size that will result in development to the west of it. In the meantime the CVG is getting no return for its heavy infrastructure investment. To trigger off the development at Alta Vista the CVG would have to take the risk of building various commercial facilities for lease or sale as has been done in some British new towns as well as in Tapiola (See pp. 64–65).

Although the urban structure of Ciudad Guayana is not a model to imitate,[33] the town is rapidly emerging as one of the most important industrial centers of Latin America. It has served its purpose as a vast laboratory of urban devel-

50

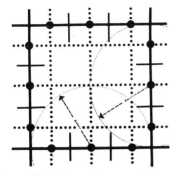

13. a. El Tablazo, Venezuela,
diagrammatic block
layout of walking
distances.

13 b. El Tablazo, Venezuela,
diagrammatic block
layout of patterns.

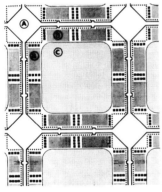

A Right of way
B Intensive development
C Squatters' reception areas

opment providing Venezuela with invaluable administrative and managerial experience which can be put to good use in the planning of further new towns such as El Tuy—a satellite of Caracas (See p. 54) and El Tablazo which is based on petrochemical industry on the east side of Lake Maracaibo.

El Tablazo El Tablazo is planned for a future population of 330,000 inhabitants. Its structure is an adaptation to a developing country of the flexible road-grid first proposed by Llewelyn-Davies and partners for the new town of Milton Keynes in England (See pp. 60–62). (Plates 73, 74) An orthogonal net of arterial roads—one km. on center—will enclose 100 ha. of "environmental areas" accommodating about 10,000 people at a gross density of 100 persons per ha. Even distribution of light industries over the town area will make them accessible on foot to many workers. This will permit a road network without grade-separated interchanges and will still assure 60 km. average speed for public transport. The model takes into account the trend toward higher car ownership in Venezuela, and is based on a "modal split" of 54 percent peak-hour trips by private car versus 46 percent by buses or jitney taxi. Within the one-km.-square environmental sectors the peripheral lots will be reserved for services and higher density controlled development (Figs. 13a, b). The central space will be available as reception areas for squatters who may form their spontaneous morphological pattern (Plates 75a, b). Such land parceling, combined with self-help housing, was pioneered in Ciudad Guayana and led to net densities of 75 persons per ha. The self-help approach liberates public funds otherwise dissipated for housing programs. It permits an underemployed person to convert his surplus energy and time into capital, by gradually improving his property. Only the essential utility lines need to be provided by the developer.

A similar land-development strategy is proposed by the same group of planners for El Tuy.

Conclusions The master plan of an industrial town must resolve the conflict between the need to maximize accessibility and the desire to minimize environmental liabilities such as pollution, noise, and accidents. This leads to greater separation of the town from heavy industry, coupled with the trend to distribute light, labor-intensive industries more evenly over the town. The allocation of land uses is often dictated by the desire to optimize traffic flow and to increase the operational efficiency of public transit systems.

Soviet practice favors higher densities to strengthen public transit. In determining density, costs must be weighed against environmental benefits: lower densities produce higher infrastructure and service costs but there may be savings in building construction. So far as there is an optimum size for the basic industry, there should be a finite size for the industrial town. In fact, in an isolated location, the town will not grow beyond a size fixed by the basic employment—unless the town acquires regional center functions in addition.

In developing countries, migration to the new town may be in excess of job provision. However the "marginals" can be absorbed in construction if traditional methods are encouraged rather then industrialized building. Labor-intensive construction combined with self-help methods can turn the building of the new town into a vast on-the-job training opportunity for the unskilled.

5 DECONGESTION

Definitions

Decongestion is the attempt to counteract the gigantism of the modern metropolis by siphoning off some of the excess population and assigning it to new communities.[1] Such policies are based on the belief that every city has its optimum size: beyond a certain "threshold" the creation of additional jobs and lodgings becomes too expensive. As Raymond Unwin stated, there is indeed "nothing gained by overcrowding."

The two sources of urban population growth are natural growth and migration: neither is easy to regulate, and police methods like enforced birth control or the internal passport system are impracticable.[2] Since unchecked growth leads to diseconomies as a result of crowding and haphazard sprawl, decongestion measures must be combined with planning intervention to assure optimum structure and land use within the metropolis.

These goals can be served by the following strategies:

1 The development of alternate growth regions

2 Satellite towns

3 Independent new towns

4 The creation of a parallel, or twin, city.

One might also include the colonial and industrial towns discussed in the previous chapters, yet a distinction should be made between towns created primarily in response to the *pull* of exploitable resources, and new towns created to decongest, in response to the *push* factor of crowding.

The growth-pole strategy has proved the most successful for deflecting migration pressure from an "overheated" region.[3] We have shown previously (chapters 2 and 3) that the magnet of a growth region can be a new capital city like Brasilia, or an industrial town like Ciudad Guyana. We shall discuss here the independent new towns, satellites, and parallel cities.

Satellite towns are comprehensively planned new communities within the metropolitan area which maintain strong functional ties with the center city. Good communications are vital and commuting time to the center should not exceed 30 to 45 minutes. Job provision need not be balanced, since the satellite profits from the job market of the metropolis. It also remains dependent on the central city for higher level services, specialty shops, cultural and entertainment facilities.

Independent new towns are deliberately located so far from the metropolis as to discourage commuting to its center. Consequently, such new towns must offer a complete range of urban activities and services. Job provision must correspond to the number of potential job seekers. Social and cultural equipment must be of sufficient variety to entice migration from the metropolis. This implies above all a large and lively town center.

Parallel cities are new towns of the same order of magnitude as the existing "twin" metropolis. The creation of a parallel city is an extreme case of decongestion which is envisaged if geographical limits of the metropolis make contiguous growth prohibitively expensive—as in Caracas or in Rio—or if water provision poses insurmountable problems, as in Mexico City or Calcutta.

The creation of such a twin city was first seriously considered in the Paris region, but the idea of the "second Paris" was abandoned in favor of the strategy of building several medium-size towns—partly because it seemed impossible to match the tradition-bound attractions of Paris in a new town built within a few decades.[4] In this respect the Brazilians seem more optimistic, since they have already embarked on the building of a "second Rio," proportioned for two or three million inhabitants. The site in the Bay of Jacarepagua is about twenty km. from the center of Rio de Janeiro but separated by the formidable barrier of the Tijuca massif. The plan by Lucio Costa (Plate 76) makes excellent use of the eighteen-km.-long oceanfront paralleled by lagoons and proposes a new center which would group the government offices of the state of Guanabara, a university, and research institutions and office buildings in the middle of the triangular site, which is as large as Rio itself.

Another parallel city in an advanced stage of planning is proposed for the decongestion of Mexico City, which suffers from the difficulties of job provision, water supply, sewage disposal, and air pollution. The plan for Ciudad Paralela, prepared by Professor Escalante,[5] accomodates three million people between Cuernavaca and Yautapec in the State of Morelos,—physically separated from the Valley of Mexico by a mountain range but to be linked by tunnels used by express trains to the capital (Plate 77). This project makes ingenious use of the sewage from Mexico City which will generate electrical energy when descending in pressure tubes from the high altitude valley; it will then be reused for agricultural irrigation around Ciudad Paralela.

Studies have also been prepared to provide for the expansion of Caracas at a site thirty km. from the capital in the El Tuy Valley,[6] and projects for parallel cities are also being examined for Tokyo, Calcutta, and other oversized metropolises. The present trend toward ever larger new towns is ironical since the modern new town policies grew out of the garden city movement, which advocated the limitation of the size of new communities to 30 to 60,000 people. We will now examine the evolution of theory and practice from garden suburbs to satellites and new towns.

From suburbs to garden cities

In the second half of the nineteenth century increased crowding and decreasing amenities made center-city living less enjoyable. This *push* factor combined with the romantic movement to make the ideal of living in a country setting highly desirable. This dream became possible for many when the railroads began to assure rapid and convenient service between the centers and their vicinity. Railroad companies rushed to promote suburban development: Le Vesinet, the first suburb of Paris, was developed in 1856 by a railroad company for its employees, but it attracted instead the upper middle classes.[7] The suburbs promised a leisurely and tranquil environment and soon acquired their own distinctive land pattern, first applied on a large scale by F. L. Olmsted in Riverside, Illinois (1869). In contrast to the grid, with its straight lines encouraging fast through traffic, Olmsted advocated a curvilinear street pattern, that produced kidney-shaped and free-form blocks.

The manifest success of railroad and trolley-suburbs inspired the first proposals for new forms of town extension. In 1882, the Spaniard, Arturo Soria y Mata, launched the idea of his linear city or *Ciudad Lineal* as large blocks of detached homes along a trolley and rail line. Ten years later his proposals became more specific: the first Linear City was to form a suburban ring around Madrid fifty km. long at a distance of about seven km. from the center, to which it would be tied by existing highways and a new subway.[8] Soria was the first to propose mass communications as the structuring spine of an entire community and he recognized the dynamic potential of his model, which could stretch from "Cadiz to St. Petersburg." In other respects the model was primitive, an undifferentiated band not unlike a tapeworm. Soria's ideas were later developed by Soviet planners (See pp. 42–45) and by Le Corbusier, but his immediate impact remained limited compared to the influence of his English contemporary, Ebenezer Howard, the father of the garden city movement.

Howard published his first tract in 1898, proposing self-contained new towns of about 30,000 inhabitants. The Garden City was to combine the "advantages of intensive urban life with the beauty and pleasures of the country." The official definition of the Garden City is a "town designed for healthy living and industry: of a size that makes possible the full measure of social life but no larger: surrounded by a rural belt—all of the land being in public ownership or held in trust for the community" (Fig. 14).[9] The city was to have sufficient employment to reduce the journey-to-work and it was to be limited to its optimum size by a permanent green belt. Howard not only had a vision of the town as an entity, but he also made meticulous calculations to prove its economic feasibility; the town would be located on cheap country land, the increment in real estate values would defray the cost of development and ultimately yield a handsome profit for the investment.

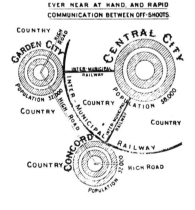

— DIAGRAM —

ILLUSTRATING CORRECT PRINCIPLE
OF A CITY'S GROWTH - OPEN COUNTRY
EVER NEAR AT HAND, AND RAPID
COMMUNICATION BETWEEN OFF-SHOOTS.

14 Diagram of Garden City by Ebenezer Howard, from *Garden Cities of Tomorrow.*

In a nutshell, Howard's theory contained key elements of the later British new town program. His contemporaries were sufficiently impressed to enable him to start his first Garden City in Letchworth in 1903 (Plate 78) [10] and a second, Welwyn, in 1919. Both are tied to London by good rail connections, yet they developed slowly since they were too expensive for workers and consequently attracted little industry at first.

The failure of Garden Cities to develop into self-contained centers may have prompted Raymond Unwin—the architect of Letchworth—to elaborate an alternative model of dormitory satellite towns surrounding an industrial center (1922) (Plate 79). In 1923 the German, E. Gloeden, went a step further, proposing a decentralized regional pattern consisting of interrelated urban cells of similar size deployed on a triangulated web of communication lines (Plate 80).[11]

On the continent, Howard's Garden City was criticized by Soria's disciples for being static and rejecting dynamic growth and by Le Corbusier for being inefficient and wasteful of the land. Corbusier asserted that low densities would "foster individualism and the downfall of collective forces" and preferred his own concept of "vertical garden cities" with "superdensities" of up to 1,000 persons per ha.

He launched the battle cry of "death to the street," putting his blocks on stilts to maximize "air, space and greenery" and the "supreme pleasure of working for the collective." This "Radiant City" concept exerted tremendous influence on later new town planning notably in its rigid segregation of functional areas; vehicular-pedestrian separation and the hierarchical ordering of the traffic system based on the speed of movement.

In America, Howard's partisans like Clarence Stein, Henry Wright, and Lewis Mumford, crusaded in favor of the garden city ideals. The rapid increase of car ownership raised the question of how to deal with the automobile. The "superblock" idea of 1923 proposed the creation of traffic-free residential environments 12 to 20 ha. by the elimination of some streets of the regular grid pattern. The area would be serviced from the periphery and street surface could be reduced by 25 percent compared to the conventional Manhattan-type grid.

Going one step further, Clarence Perry advocated self-contained neighborhoods of 5,000 people with a community center, schools, and other institutions in the center—within four minutes walk from any building (Fig. 15). Perry looked at the neighborhood as a small-scale social unit that would foster local initiative and restore democratic participation to a level that characterized the small New England villages.[12]

A further refinement was popularized by the first American garden city: Radburn planned by Stein and Wright. The town was planned in 1928 to contain 25,000 people in three neighborhoods, but the Depression prevented the full success of the undertaking. Yet the one completed neighborhood sufficed to demonstrate the value of the "Radburn pattern"—

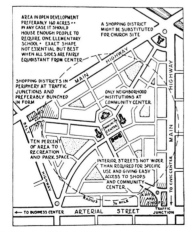

15 Plan of "neighborhood" idea by Clarence Perry, 1929.

an ingenious device for the horizontal separation of pedestrian and vehicular areas. Cul-de-sac alleys serving a cluster of twenty houses interpenetrate with garden strips in a cogwheel fashion and the green strips connect with a large commons in the center of the superblock.

A number of greenbelt towns were founded in the U.S.A. around 1933 as a result of the New Deal policy of trying to provide useful work for men on unemployment relief. Although these towns remained small (3,000 to 7,000 inhabitants) and lacked industry, they further popularized key elements of the garden city concept in America.

On a more important scale, the 1926 regional plan for New York State prepared by Henry Wright suggested a balanced distribution of population and industry by the creation of new towns. However, such a concept was too far ahead of political development to be acceptable, and the first demonstration of a new town policy on a regional scale had to wait until the 1940s. When it came, it happened in Britain rather then the United States.

The British new towns

The British new town policy is based on a comprehensive planning legislation which evolved gradually by a process of public discussion and advocacy. In this the Garden City Association played a key role. Founded in 1899 by E. Howard, and later renamed the *Town and Country Planning Association,* it consistently opposed the addition of further suburbs to large cities and lobbied in favor of decongestion by the creation of new towns.

In 1940 the Barlow Commission examined the distribution of the industrial population and concluded that further growth of industry in London must be restricted. Three years later, Patrick Abercrombie suggested for the first time that limits could be imposed on density within the County of London and that suburban sprawl could be stopped by establishing a permanent greenbelt around the built-up area.[13] His *Greater London Plan of 1944* set the maximum density at 250 persons per ha. (100 people per acre) This implied that an "overspill" population of well over a million people would need to be relocated from the "inner ring" around London and consequently called for the immediate creation of ten new towns beyond the greenbelt. Wartime discipline and the shell-shock of the blitz may have contributed to the public acceptance of so drastic a proposal.

In 1945 the government appointed a new committee, with Lord Reith as chairman, to elaborate proposals for the new towns. The Reith Committee suggested that the new towns should be self-contained rather then satellites: to be located 40 to 50 km. from London and to have populations of 20–60,000. The Committee established the doctrine that the new towns should be built by government appointed development corporations rather then by local authorities, commercial builders, or nonprofit associations. Once completed, the new towns would gradually become self-governing. *The New Town Act of 1946* gave the secretaries of state power to designate any area of land—including existing towns or villages—as the site of a new town and to appoint development corporations. A New Town Corporation is a public agency with powers of eminent domain but otherwise acting as would a private developer—borrowing money at current interest rates and trying to show a profit on the long term.

It is convenient to group the British new towns into three "generations," corresponding to three distinct stages of the development of the theory.

The *first generation* includes fourteen New Towns designated before 1950. Eight of them were intended to draw industry and population from London.[14] The planning of these towns was strongly influenced by Garden City philosophy and concern for an "English way of life," in which F. Gibberd included "segregation of home and work, a preference for openness, and a home with a private garden." The resulting plans were characterized by low densities and emphasis on self-contained, intraverted neighborhoods.

Stevenage was the first new town to be designated on a site of 2,440 ha., 55 km. north of London. The plan placed the town center next to the railroad station, and provided a single large industrial area on the other side of the tracks. The original six neighborhoods were grouped in a fan shape around the town center—each sector focused on a sizable subcenter of its own. Due to the very low density of 85 persons per ha., the outlying areas are more then two miles from the center—too far for pedestrians. The town center, which was finished in 1962, sported the first entirely pedestrian precinct in England and it soon acquired regional importance (Plate 81).[15] The town was originally planned for 60,000 people but the target was revised upward to 105,000 in 1966, which called for extensive modifications in the road system, including the extension of the commercial core into areas originally reserved for warehousing, the building of grade-separated interchanges, and of multilevel parking decks to accomodate 7,000 cars (Plate 82).

Harlow is perhaps the most successful of the first generation towns. Planned by Frederick Gibberd on a handsome site of 2,500 ha., it has a very systematic hierarchical internal structure. Gibberd divided the town area into four sectors separated by green wedges. Each sector consists of three to four neighborhoods of 5,000 to 6,000 persons (Fig. 16). In addition to the neighborhood centers, there are also intermediate-sized centers serving each sector; together these subcenters contain as many shops as there are in the main town center. This center offers a high quality of equipment: it has a theater, a bowling alley, and is embellished by numerous excellent statues. Like Stevenage, Harlow was to have a population of 60,000 but in 1973 it was decided to enlarge the population to 123,000 by densification and by adding six new neighborhoods. Higher density is achieved by providing 20 percent of the dwelling units in apartments;

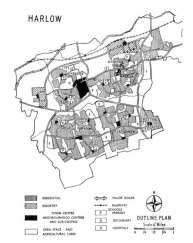

HARLOW

RESIDENTIAL

INDUSTRY

TOWN CENTRE
NEIGHBOURHOOD CENTRES
AND SUB-CENTRES

OPEN SPACE AND
AGRICULTURAL LAND

MAJOR ROADS

RAILWAYS

SCHOOLS
P PRIMARY

S SECONDARY

H HOSPITALS

N

OUTLINE PLAN
Scale of Miles
0 ¼ ½ ¾ 1

16 Schematic plan of Harlow, England by Frederick Gibberd, 1948.

against only 10 percent of apartments in Stevenage. There is a very good variety of housing including experimental types like the Bishopsfield "Casbah," 1966, (Plate 83) with a carpet-type pattern and parking placed under a central plaza.

The aerial photograph (Plate 84) shows the industrial park and the adjacent Mark Hall area with the subcenter of the NE quarter. The Great Parndon area in the SW quarter (Plate 85a) is an example of the mix of older and newer housing patterns, including the "Casbah." [16]

Some shortcomings of the first generation town plans soon came in for sharp criticism: the low densities and overly generous provision of greenery resulted in high infrastructure cost and were blamed for lack of visual variety and animation. The multiplication of subcenters sapped the vitality of the town center. The original target population of 60,000 people proved to be too small to support a sufficient variety of cultural and entertainment facilities. At the same time the rise in car ownership increased the demand for parking space and garages. All this combined to favor the increase of the target population and an enlargement of the centers, but the nucleated plans made modifications costly.

Trying a new tack, the *second generation* plans—which originated between 1950–1960—tried to foster "urbanity" with compactness and higher densities, and strengthened the dominance of the town center in the composition.

In the study for the town of Hook, the Garden City emphasis on self-contained neighborhoods was rejected and housing was tightly integrated with the center. Hook has a single linear core with housing densities highest in the central area at 250 persons per ha. and decreasing toward the periphery: 175 persons per ha. in the intermediate zone and 100 persons per ha. in the outer zone. This assures that three-fifths of the town's residents would live within a seven minute walk from the center. Plate 86 shows the pedestrian-way system connecting the center with the residential zones and leading to the green open spaces beyond. The separation of pedestrian and vehicular traffic is total, and the center is highly accessible to cars but not dominated by them. To avoid a center ringed by parking, as in Stevenage or Harlow, the center of Hook is placed on the top of multilevel parking and the service roads. Plate 87 shows the ingenious primary and secondary road system. Although Hook was never built, the publication of the seminal study was widely acclaimed, and the principles set forth in the Hook study were tested in practice with the construction of the new town of Cumbernauld.

Cumbernauld, twenty km. from Glasgow, was planned for 70,000 people. Like Hook it is a compact town with a linear core. A hill ridge four km. long and 1.5 km. wide is occupied by a multilevel center which sits astride the town expressway. The town was to form a single entity—without any distinct neighborhoods—and housing is tightly linked to the center by pedestrianways (Plate 88). With 205 persons per ha., Cumbernauld has the highest gross density among British new towns: 40 percent of all dwelling units are apartments. Buildings are grouped to form enclosed courts to provide wind protection and the pedestrian paths pass right under the buildings. In contrast to the first generation towns which tried to revive the open market square, the center of Cumbernauld derives from the covered shopping arcades of the nineteenth century. This shopping arcade occupies the second level of a deliberately complex structure with a bus terminal and vast parking facilities on its lower level. In search for a greater activity mix, some decorative duplex apartments have also been integrated into the "megastructure" (Plates 89, 90).[17]

For all its interest the concept of Cumbernauld proved rather inflexible: when the target population of the town was enlarged, two new housing areas had to be added which are rather cut off from the town center, and consequently had to be equipped with neighborhood centers. Among the new towns of Britain, Cumbernauld remains the single example of a compact town although it influenced the design of the London County Council's Thamesmead Development (Plate 91). This is a "new town-in-town" scheme for 60,000 persons, located within the County of London area.

Thamesmead is not a new town in the strict British sense, since it does not serve the purpose of decongestion. Yet its structure—consisting of linear, high-density sinews—offers a novel environment which will be emulated elsewhere if it finds popular acceptance (Plates 92, 93).

Another heuristic study—related to Hook and Cumbernauld—was the first proposal for Milton Keynes prepared by F. B. Pooley in 1964. Located halfway between London and Birmingham, Milton Keynes is destined to become one of the largest new towns in Britain with a future population of 250,000. Pooley located his town center on the north-south axis between the existing towns of Wolverton and Bletchley and proposed a city form consisting of four east-west strips each containing 55,000 people, served by two monorail loops (Plate 94). The linear strips were to be formed by a series of townships of 5,000 people around monorail stations (Plate 95). Each township would include some land reserved for light industry while heavy industry was assigned to the east and west edges of the site. This imaginative plan failed to clear the County Council, and in 1966 when the Ministry attempted to designate the proposed 10,000 ha., opposition forced the amputation of 1,200 ha. leading to a restudy of the basic concept.

The 1967 plan for Runcorn by Professor Arthur Ling is related to the Pooley plan of Milton Keynes—insofar as the town structure is determined by the public transit system (Plate 96). Runcorn is on the river Mersey, twenty km. from Liverpool, and it was designated in 1964 with an area of 2,925 ha. The site included sizable developed areas with 30,000 residents. The ingenious town structure is in the form of two rings served by a figure-eight bus loop, the whole

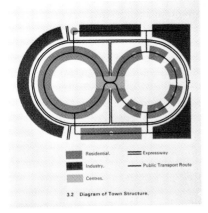

Residential. ══ Expressway
Industry. —— Public Transport Route
Centres.

3.2 Diagram of Town Structure.

7 Diagram of Runcorn town
structure, 1967.

surrounded by an expressway (Fig. 17). Residential sectors
concentrate around bus stops located every 800 m. The buses
use their own reserved right-of-way. The town structure is
maximizing the attraction of public transport to which 50
percent of the peak hour trips have been assigned, resulting
in a great reduction in demand for parking space around
the center. The radius of a five-minute walk from the bus
stops, and a fixed gross density of 175 persons per ha. yields
a development unit of 8,000 persons, deployed in four clusters
of 2,000 people served by an elementary school (Plate 97).
This suggests a return to the neighborhood concept. The
town center groups 60 percent of commerce with offices and
cultural and entertainment areas. It sits atop parking decks
for 4,500 cars. Surrounded by traffic it is more insular than
the center of Cumbernauld (Plates 98, 99).

A community structure similar to Runcorn is proposed for
the Scottish new town of Irvine. This town has a unique
seaside location forty km. from Glasgow. Designated in 1966,
it is planned to grow to 140,000 residents by 1986. The size
of residential units is determined by walking distance from
the bus stops (Plate 100). Unit size is 4,000 people, and two
units are grouped around a secondary school (Plate 101).
The most interesting feature of the plan is the town center,
consisting of a 300 m. long linear shopping deck which will
link the railroad station, across the river Irvine, with the
center of the old city and may be prolonged toward the
west all the way to the waterfront on Irvine Bay.

Although public transport shaped the town structure of
Runcorn, in general the *third generation* town plans reflect
the desire to optimize the full use of the private automobile.
A nonhierarchical, homogeneous town structure is sought
by the dispersal of traffic-generating elements. The goal is
to provide equal accessibility to all points and equal choice
to all residents "striking a new balance between home, work
and leisure." This concept was first propagated by the
American, Melvin Webber,[18] and quickly espoused by traffic
planners like Colin Buchanan. In his 1965 Southampton study,
Buchanan proposed a reticulated road net formed by a
double road-grid, alternating public highways and local roads
two km. apart.

In their 1966 plan for the new town of Washington, Llewelyn-
Davies and Partners used a similar reticulated system. To
avoid tidal traffic loads, industry is distributed over the town
area. Although the grid streets enclose sectors of 4,500
people, these are not meant to be socially coherent units
like neighborhoods. The actual plan for Milton Keynes by the
same designers (Llewelyn-Davies, et al.) carries these ideas
one step further. The most "American" of British new towns,
Milton Keynes, will consist 50 percent of privately owned
homes, and proposes to be leisurely dispersed "yet urban
in the level of opportunities." This is to be accomplished by
an efficient one-km. grid of major roadways enclosing development islands of 100 ha. Midblock access points will
coincide with bus stops and pedestrian underpasses. Plate

61

102 shows the strategic plan with the even distribution of employment sites and the reticulated grid with its midblock activity nodes. Contradicting the goal of homogeneity, a major regional center is proposed to take up two and a half grid squares (Plate 103). The plan allocates 250,000 future residents with the low density of 100 persons per ha.; but the scale certainly got out of hand because some grid squares are as far as four miles from the town center. To ensure the young, old, and invalids of public transport, a dial-a-bus system is proposed, yet the economic feasibility of such a system is still unproven.

An enormous capital investment budget of 1.75 billion dollars will permit experiments with innovative systems in health care and in social development. There will be an attempt to control the mix of population groups and to integrate a fixed percentage of racial minorities and hard-core unemployables into the town population.

Town promotional literature makes much of low densities boasting that "the greatest achievement would be to drive through and never know you have been there"—yet this return to the sprawl of the first generation towns is already much criticized for wasting land and for serving more the needs of the automobile than of the pedestrian.[19]

It is fair to say that the twenty-five years of British new town experience represent a considerable success. Building new towns has become a national policy that transcends changes of government. The population of new towns is now around 1.6 million and by the end of the century an estimated 3.5 million people will live in them in an environment of high quality. The geographer, Peter Hall, demonstrated, however, that the new towns did not stop the growth of the London metropolis.

Although London sprawl has stopped at the greenbelt, the creation of the new towns contributed to a tremendous densification in the outer ring area. This insight has recently led to greater emphasis on the development of new towns in lagging regions and to the designation of new sites at distances of 100 km. and more from London.

Satellite towns

Scandinavia Five years after the publication of the Greater London Plan Swedish planners proposed the building of satellite towns around Stockholm tied to the creation of new subway lines. This was to be an undertaking of lesser scope than in England, appropriate to the scale of the Stockholm region. The satellites were never envisaged as self-contained. As integral elements of Greater Stockholm they have the function of decongesting the center and providing an orderly framework for the growth of the region. There was no need for special legislation, since public ownership of land offered unique opportunities. Since 1637 Stockholm had a planning commission which early embarked on systematic land acquisition. By 1964, 70 percent of the city area was in public ownership and by 1971 the city also owned land reserves of 50,000 ha. beyond its boundaries.[20] In 1971 city and county were fusioned to form Greater Stockholm which contains one-fifth of the Swedish population.

The 1950 plan proposed satellite towns of 50,000 people, each to consist of three to four neighborhoods clustered around a subway station. The location of the satellites was determined by the subway lines and the condition that commuting time to center Stockholm should not exceed thirty minutes. Neighborhood size and density were fixed by the rule that the majority of dwellings should be within a 500 m. radius from subway stops. With neighborhood populations ranging from 7,000 to 15,000 people, fairly high densities resulted. This accounts for the fact that 75 percent of all dwelling units are rental apartments compared to 10 percent in Stevenage and 40 percent in Cumbernauld. Each neighborhood has its subcenter, but a major town center is also provided. In general, the development of the satellites was perfectly coordinated with the completion of the subway stations, but the opening of the town centers fell behind schedule and caused some hardship to the first residents.

Vällingby—the first of the satellites to be built—has a community structure reminiscent of Harlow: it consists of five large neighborhoods each with its own center, composed of smaller groups of 2,000 to 3,000 people focused on a school and local shops (Plate 104). The town center opened in 1954 with a generous pedestrian mall placed atop the subway station and truck service areas (Plate 105). Vällingby has at present a population of 63,000 persons. Since the center also attracts shoppers from the surrounding region, the original parking provision of 600 cars soon proved inadequate, yet enlargement of the center is hampered by the tight grouping of apartment buildings.

The Farsta group was planned in 1953 and occupation started four years later. There are six neighborhoods, somewhat smaller then in Vällingby, containing about 7,000 people. Since it has been established that the satellite centers must also serve a regional function, the center of Farsta is surrounded by parking lots for 1,500 cars, which isolate it from its surroundings. In the case of the third satellite Skärholmen—destined to be a service center for 250,000 people, the parking provision again had to be raised to 4,000 places.

This first generation of satellites became well known for the romantic grouping of their buildings, adapted to the natural landscape of trees, rocks, and water. Later models show a marked departure from the romantic pattern and are both denser and more geometrical in their layout.

The plan of Täby is a formalistic although pleasing exercise, with circular segments (Plate 106). Tensta-Rinkeby and Norra Järvafaltet have linear plans and a more austere orthogonal pattern.

A new scale is introduced in Järvafaltet which will occupy the former exercise ground of the Stockholm military garrison, a site of 5,000 ha. Although only ten to fifteen km.

from Stockholm, Järva is destined to become a full scale regional center with a population of 100,000 and will offer jobs for 70,000 people, more than are needed for its active population.

Norra Järvafaltet—the first development unit—is being built for 30,000 people. Its master plan—approved in 1970—is related to the concepts of Hook and Cumbernauld in rejecting the principle of neighborhoods and focal centers in favor of a linear plan. A pedestrian mall and service spine link three subway stations, paralleled by a strip of housing groups which permits the preservation of a single large recreation area. A town expressway separates the town from its large industrial park.

This recent trend toward more geometric layouts expresses the Swedish commitment to industrialized building methods, in contrast to England where conventional construction is still favored in new towns. Unlike the new towns around London which offer abundant industrial employment, the Stockholm satellites made insufficient provisions for industrial sites and there has been a lack of incentives to attract industry. This combined with the fact that the town centers offer only a few office jobs, explains that in Vällingby or Farsta every second active person commutes to the center of Stockholm and only one in five finds his job within his community.

Tapiola—the first satellite town of Helsinki—offers a more balanced model: although the residents can profit from job opportunities in Helsinki, it is proposed to match employment provision with the demand. Tapiola is located on an inlet of the Gulf of Finland, less then ten km. from the center of Helsinki, but geographically separated from the capital by the Bay. It is a relatively small town, planned for a fixed size of 4,758 dwelling units or a population of 17,000, but it is the nucleus of a larger town of 80,000 (Plate 107). The town is built with a very low density of 75 persons per ha. in a parklike setting of fields, forests, and water (Plate 108). There are three neighborhoods, characterized by the consistent mix of multistory and low-rise buildings. This disposition fosters casual social intercourse between the residents, composed 42 percent of blue-collar workers and 58 percent of professional and managerial groups. 90 percent of the dwelling units are privately owned, which implies that the blue-collar component consists of skilled workers. The lowest income groups are not represented. The multipurpose town center groups an astonishing variety of urban amenities. The design is the outcome of a 1953 competition won by Aarne Ervi who made excellent use of an old quarry, turning it into a reflecting pool as the center of a building group including a church, a swimming hall, community theater, and library in addition to the commercial center. The group is dominated by a landmark office building with a restaurant and a beacon on the top (Plate 109). The center will be expanded in two stages to the seashore and will in the future include underground parking and a subway station.

Curiously, the fact that the subway does not yet exist, and connections to Helsinki are far from ideal, may have boosted the town center, since the relative isolation produced a demonstrable need for local cultural and sports facilities.

Unlike British or Swedish new towns Tapiola was built by a private, nonprofit organization without government support and against some official obstruction. In fact, the town owes its existance to the energy and ability of a single individual—Heikki von Hertzen—who in 1951 convinced a number of trade unions and welfare organizations to finance the building of Tapiola as a joint venture. Von Hertzen views the creation of Tapiola as the first step in an ambitious regional development program. His "Seven Cities" proposal of 1964 offers an alternative to the official "amoeba" plan for the Helsinki region, which envisages the growth of the capital to 1.5 million people by 1990. In contrast, Von Hertzen proposes to limit central Helsinki to 630,000 persons and the metropolitan area to 1,300,000 and to organize regional growth in seven new towns.

The success of Tapiola encouraged the development corporation Asuntosaatio to make reality of the Seven-Cities plan by acquiring land for two further new towns located on the westerly growth axis from the capital; Espoo Bay, eighteen km. from Helsinki, will be a twin city developed around lagoons, with a population of 110,000 persons; and Porkkala, 61 km. from Helsinki, a maritime center of 200,000.

In promoting his new towns, Von Hertzen ran up against the prejudice that new towns are a bad risk for investment. To build key elements of the Tapiola center Asuntosaatio had to provide the financing, build and operate a swimming hall, department store, hotel, and so forth, as demonstration projects—being able to lease or sell the facilities only after they had proved their viability. This imaginative and courageous approach by private development remains unmatched in Europe but it has become an inspiration to the developers of new communities in the United States.

Japan The European experiments with decongestion have been followed closely in Japan, where the proposal of a "Greater Tokyo Plan" complete with greenbelt and British-type new towns was followed by the construction of several satellite towns on the Swedish model.[21] Two such satellites, Senri and Senboku have recently been completed in the Osaka area. They were built from 1963 to 1970 as a joint venture of the Prefectural Government and the Japanese Housing Corporation: although planned as dormitory towns to take the overspill population from Osaka, with populations of 150,000 persons they are far too large to remain oversized housing projects.

Senri, located seventeen km. west of Osaka, is tied to the center city by two rapid transit rail lines and two expressways. It consists largely of prefabricated apartment buildings grouped into neighborhoods of 10 to 12,000 people. The town area of 3,000 ha. is rather small for the population, although gross density does not exceed 125 persons per ha. (Plates 110, 111). The town center includes some office employment but lacks industry. However, the town has a land reserve in the 326-ha.-site of the 1970 International Exposition, which also left some permanent monuments (a museum and fountains) to be integrated into future development. A unique opportunity was missed with the demolition of the multispeed movement system of Expo. This system, which consisted of a peripheral monorail and arterial elevated speedwalks, could have provided the basic structure of an exciting new regional center. However, the site is large enough to accommodate a university with 50,000 students, and the decision to build it on the Expo site provides Senri with a "town forming" employment base which it needs to acquire identity.

Since the congestion of the largest Japanese cities is becoming intolerable, one may look forward to a more comprehensive, regional approach in the planning of new towns and satellites. The Japanese are still trying to find their own style in new town building which may lead them to attempt very large new towns of the one million population range. Such a town is now being proposed to decongest Tokyo by the removal of government functions and the transfer of the large universities.[22] The success of the Japanese new towns and satellites will undoubtedly influence planners in other Asiatic countries, where the extremely rapid growth of the largest cities will soon require decongestion measures.

Russia In Russia, the growth of Moscow early focused interest on decentralization with the building of satellites or *goroda sputniki*.[23] The 1935 Moscow General Plan limited future population to five million and imposed strict controls on migration to the city. Nevertheless, by 1959 the target size had been surpassed by the actual population. In 1960 annexation of the suburban areas brought the size of Moscow to six million.

The city proper is limited by a ring expressway completed in 1962 with a radius of about eighteen km. from the center. Beyond this boundary a wide greenbelt is being preserved although it contains numerous *dachas,* and older planned satellite towns—like Elekrostal, Khimky, and Krasnogarsk—which send hundreds of thousands of daily commuters to Moscow (Plate 112).[24] New satellites are to be located beyond the greenbelt; Kryukovo, forty-one km. from the center along the railline to Leningrad, is nearing completion.

Soviet theory postulates the integral unity of the city and its metropolitan area which should also form a single administrative entity.

Within a metropolitan region, the geographer Afitchenko [25] identifies three types of satellites, that differ in their degree of employment provision—ranging from self-contained towns to dormitory suburbs—and he correlates their degree of dependency with their distance from the central city. Distances ranging forty to eighty km. from the center are considered optimal: such distances discourage commuting yet the residents can still profit from the unique cultural amenities and sports facilities of the central city. With respect to employment, the self-contained towns are preferred to dormitory communities. According to Baranov the optimum size of satellites lies between 50,000 and 100,000 persons. It is defined as the size where the overall cost of construction per head of population can be kept below the cost per head in the parent city.[26]

The Russians claim to have learned from the British experience, where the total mass of new towns around London proved insufficient to balance the pull of the metropolis: their 1956 regional scheme for Moscow proposes a more adequate "counterbalancing mass" of twenty new towns with a total population of one million; one-fifth of the number of residents in the center city.

It is interesting to observe that even in the Soviet Union an increasing number of satellites are built around a "postindustrial" type of employment base consisting of teaching and research facilities. These include Zhukovsky, Sumgait, Dubna, Akademgorodok near Novosibirsk, and Sestroretsk near Leningrad.

Surprisingly, for a planned society, there are gaps between theory and practice in the USSR. Planning and implementation are divorced. In the Moscow region, the Institute for the General Plan is responsible for the preparation of pilot plans but more detailed plans are developed independently by the Moscow State Building Institute: MOSSTROI. Horizontal coordination between various ministries and authorities suffers from contradictory interests, and the priority accorded to production encourages among managers of industrial enterprises a cavalier attitude toward the planning goals —facts that are frequently criticized in the Soviet press.

French *villes nouvelles*

France awoke late to the need to control the growth of Paris, and the building of new towns was not seriously proposed until 1965. Yet Paris is certainly the most overcrowded metropolis of the Western world: in 1962 nearly three million Parisians lived in a municipal area of only 10,500 ha.—half the size of the city of Stockholm. The average gross density of Paris is more then double the density of inner London and in some districts reaches 1,000 persons per ha.

Although discussion of decentralization started after the war, at first all energies were absorbed by the postwar housing crisis: a staggering shortage arose, made worse by substandard housing stock, half of which required replacement.[27] As a first response, the building of *grands ensembles,* or public housing estates, was rushed without much regard for sound location or quality.

The average scale of these estates was around 500 rental units but the scale jumped in 1958 with the ZUP (*Zones à Urbaniser en Priorité*) legislation which designated hundreds of zones for priority development. Some ZUP projects were very large—Créteuil, near Paris, has a planned population of 60,000; Toulouse-Le Mirail 100,000—yet they are oversized housing projects rather then genuine new communities.[28] By 1964 the various *grands ensembles* housed two million people, half of them jammed in the suburban ring of Paris. Such projects were often located at random on any available land without good access to jobs and without adequate shopping and sociocultural equipment. Such errors proved difficult to correct since most projects were too small to justify the addition of town centers, and in any case no land had been reserved for such development.

A first Master Plan of the Paris region—PADOG (*Plan d'Aménagement et d'Organisation Générale de la Region Parisienne*)—was launched in 1960. Its intent was to halt the physical growth of Paris by promoting eight provincial cities as counterbalance nodes—or *métropoles d'équilibre.* This proposal rejected the possibility of creating new towns, on the assumption that they would increase the pull of the Paris region. Yet the PADOG measures proved inadequate, and in 1965 when the regional population hit nine million, a new regional Master Plan was revealed. It is based on the premise that if the Paris region is permitted to grow at the same rate as other French towns, the population would double from nine to eighteen million before the year 2000. The plan then normatively sets the year 2000 population of the Paris region at fourteen million people, making the heroic assumption that migration to Paris can be cut to zero while the growth rate of other French towns is increased two or three-fold during the planning period.

This still left the planners with the task of creating two million new jobs and allocating space for five million more people which led to the recommendation of five new towns with a population of about 500,000. This is a radical departure from PADOG and its rejection of new towns; it parallels the Soviet concept of "adequate counterbalance mass": half of the region's projected population growth is assigned to the new towns which together will have to absorb 2.5 million people! These towns are key elements of a proposed linear growth pattern along an east-west "preferential axis" on both sides of the Marne and the upper Seine (Plate 113). The five new towns designated are Evry and Melun-Senart to the south, St. Quentin-en-Yvelines to the southwest, Marne-la-Vallée toward the east, and Cergy-Pontoise to the northwest of Paris. These towns are located only twenty to thirty km. from central Paris and they will be neither satellites nor fully independent. Their rasion d'être is to break the monocentrism of Paris and by drawing employment out of the center city reduce commuting and relieve traffic congestion.

To give each town a sharply distinct profile the definition of a different vocation for each is attempted (in the proposed land-use mix and town structure). In contrast to the gloomy *grands ensembles,* priority is given to the development of lively centers, which is justifiable, since the new towns are by no means located on virgin land but in the midst of rapidly urbanizing areas. The new centers will reorient and restructure these disorderly agglomerations. At the same time great emphasis is laid on the development of leisure areas: Marne-la-Vallée will profit from its riverside; Melun from the shorelines of the Seine; Cergy, the loop of the Oise; St. Quentin from its marshland; and Evry will have its artificial lake. Good ties to Paris are considered vital: Marne-la-Vallée is located on planned extensions of the regional express-subway and will be structured like the Swedish satellites in segments focusing on subway stations. Evry will be connected to the dynamic new business center of Paris at the Défense by a monorail using a revolutionary air-cushion vehicle.

The theory that the growth of the Paris region could be checked only if the growth rate of the counterbalance cities is accelerated, led in 1966 to the formation of the first OREAM (*Organisation d'Etudes d'Aménagement des Aires Metropolitaines*)—or metropolitan planning teams. These soon proposed the development of satellite towns related to the large provincial cities of Rouen, Lille, Lyon, and Marseille. These satellites will have to be kept on a modest scale to avoid weakening the traditional central role of their parent cities. At the same time the small size of these provincial new towns permits their use to test various innovative proposals.

The first of these satellites to be designated, in 1967, was Le Vaudreuil, twenty km. southwest of Rouen, located in a bend of the Seine river. The site has great recreational potential but it is near the polluted Rouen area; hence it was decided to use the new town as a laboratory for pollution control. All design elements are evaluated for their environmental impact. Another novel idea is to create from the beginning a complete urban entity, the "seed" of the future town of 150,000. This seed of 15,000 people is not meant to be one of several future neighborhoods, but a miniature city containing all urban activities and capable of continuous growth.

L'Isle d'Abeu, the satellite of Lyon, is linked to the new international airport as its employment base. Its target size is 150,000 people but alternate strategies have been prepared to reduce its size to 80,000—or alternately to enlarge it to 250,000—depending on the dynamism manifested in its first stage of growth.

Villeneuve d'Asq is to be built only eight km. from the center of Lille and will be tied to a new university with 20,000 students.

The planning of a fourth new town imposed itself as the result of the creation of the vast port and industrial complex on the Bay of Fos near Marseilles: 60,000 new industrial jobs will attract half a million new residents to the area. To avoid random urbanization, a ring-shaped new town is being proposed around the Étang de Berre, yet the opposition of local groups has so far prevented comprehensive development.

Here we may note a curious paradox: the decongestion of Paris depends on the success of the policy to foster the growth of the large provincial cities: the satellite towns are supposedly the instruments for achieving this goal, yet little progress is made in building them, while the large new towns of the Paris region are rapidly becoming a reality. The simultaneous building of these large towns calls for tremendous initial investment and the coordination of innumerable public agencies and private enterprise.

Cergy-Pontoise may serve as an example for the sequence of actions involved. The planning team was recruited in 1966. Three years later the Master Plan was ready, land acquisition and infrastructure development were completed. Since the site included parts of five political communes, these had to be persuaded to form an Intercommunal Syndicate. The development corporation—or *Etablissement Public*—was organized in 1970 and the Intercommunal Master Plan of fifteen communes approved in 1971 (Plate 114). Cergy will accommodate 380,000 newcomers and offer 150,000 jobs including 60,000 places in offices in two different centers. The horseshoe-shaped town of five residential sectors will hug the peninsula formed by a loop of the Oise river. The peninsula is developed as a leisure park with marina facilities, accessible to cars but not crossed by any vehicular traffic.

The British experience proved that industry can easily be enticed to relocate to new towns, but it is difficult to attract sufficient office employment. Aware of this, the planners of Cergy were determined to assure the success of the town within the critical initial time span of five years and they included a sizable civic center in the first development phase (Plate 115). This strategy proved phenomenally successful, and a business district grew rapidly around the futuristic "Préfecture"—seat of the county government (Plates 116, 117).

The major town center—proposed on a site four km. farther away—may be less successful, since it will have to assert itself against the primacy of the civic center. Experience in Ciudad Guayana (Plate 68–70, Fig. 12), Beer Sheba (Plates 52, 53) and elsewhere showed how difficult it is to create a viable major center in face of the competition of an already established vigorous subcenter.

To avoid such a predicament, the new town of Evry proposes the alternative of concentrating all center-seeking functions in a large single mass. Evry is located on the most dynamic growth axis of the Paris region, along the A6 Southern expressway. The new town will give focus to a rapidly urbanizing area which includes numerous vast housing projects. The future "catchment area" of Evry will contain more then half a million people.

The center of Evry is confined between the expressway and the community route No. 7 paralleling the Seine (Plate 118). It is being built over a complex utility tunnel system, a unique type of infrastructure. A bridgelike Préfecture (Plate 116) is the core of the civic center. A transportation node, a giant commercial center, and a technical university will all be tied to a highly unusual multipurpose "Agora" which will integrate under one roof a variety of social and cultural activities without strict spatial separation. This is a courageous experiment, since the marshaling of multifarious public and private participants is attempted on an unprecedented scale. The center will radiate four swastikalike branches, each consisting of a public transit line—using its own right-of-way as in Runcorn—paralleled by a pedestrian corridor lined by shops and high density housing (Plate 118). Evry will be built in three phases, starting with a first sector of 7,000 dwelling units to the north of the center. The design for this first phase or "Evry 1" was selected by a competition among architect-developer teams, which yielded several innovative projects. The winning design is composed of residential "hills." The need for surface parking is eliminated with the residents' garages disposed in the interior of the pyramids. Another project put forward the even more daring —and costly—concept of a single seventeen-story continuous megastructure, saving three-fourths of the available site for recreation space. Such projects point toward urban forms which may well characterize future new towns in crowded areas—and offer the greatest contrast to land-wasting low-density models like the American new towns or Milton Keynes.

New towns for America

From the historian's standpoint one may argue that most American cities originated as "new towns," yet planned new communities in the modern sense are a recent phenomenon on the American scene. Reasons for this late start are the traditional commitment to free enterprise coupled with prejudice against all forms of planning, and the preference for a pragmatic rather then a theoretical approach.

In contrast to Europe where new town building was preceded by ideological debate and comprehensive legislation, the embryonic new town acts of the U.S. emerge with undue delay after the seminal thrusts of private development. The American way to success by trial and error proceeded by the gradual amalgamation of disparate elements that have proved their popular appeal: the low density suburb; the car-oriented shopping center; the industrial park; the country-club; and the exurban university campus. Curiously, this disjointed approach gave us a variety of prototypes for a new kind of postindustrial community—no longer based on industrial employment, or in any case not to the same extent as the European new towns. The American model has a predominantly "tertiary" employment base of offices, research, teaching, etc., and is geared to the consumption of goods and services. Depending on varying emphases in the activity-mix we may identify four distinct types:

1 The leisure-oriented "country-club community"

2 "The city of efficient consumption" [29] with a giant shopping center as its heart

3 The new town, focused on education and research, with a large university as its "industry"

4 Specialized communities: resort and gambling towns; "Disney-Worlds"; "adult-oriented" and senior-citizen settlements which are town-sized fully planned communities equipped with all social and technical amenities but signally lacking any kind of "productive" employment (productive in the Marxist sense of producing agricultural or manufactured goods)

This interpretation of present trends calls for a brief summary of the evolution that led from thoughtless, giant subdivisions to such model communities as Columbia, Md.

In the United States postwar housing shortage was met by large-scale tract development with little concern beyond offering "a good home for a good price." The new mobility gained by wide automobile ownership encouraged urban sprawl and the middle class left the city in search of a new way of life in the suburbs. Retail business followed its customers and gave rise to the suburban shopping center, accessible only by private automobile.

Since industry also tended to seek exurban location, the ensuing competition for developable land led to the familiar crazy-quilt of suburban land use. As shopping centers grew in size they attracted offices, entertainment, motels, and became the focus of the unstructured "noncommunity." [30] Developers of shopping centers became aware of the fact that the centers created inflated land values all around: to avoid unsightly parasite developments around their centers—but mostly to capture the appreciated land values—the promoters started to buy up much more land than needed for the center and thus became involved with land planning of the surrounding area. At the same time the tract developers, having satisfied the urgent housing needs, were looking for something new for the more discriminating customer and came up with the "packaged community"—a more completely equipped suburb, offering recreation areas, shopping, and offices in addition to the homes. The converging interests of tract developers and the promoters of shopping centers created the prototype suburban community focused on a giant shopping center, misleadingly marketed as a "new town." In the absence of regional planning, the location of such developments was determined by market forces or the whim of the developer. The dawn of a new era was signaled, however, in 1961 by the "Year 2000" regional plan for Washington D.C., which not only proposed a pattern for orderly growth but actually pinpointed favorable sites for the location of new towns (Plate 119). Imaginative developers took up the challenge: the first two new towns to deserve this name, Reston, Va., and Columbia, Md. became reality.[31]

Reston is 23 km. west of Washington on one of the development axes proposed by the "Year 2000" plan. There, the developer R. E. Simon acquired 2,872 ha. One-fifth has been set aside for recreational use, the rest will accomodate a target population of 75,000 people at the very low density of 34 persons per ha. The concept of Reston is unabashedly oriented toward a leisure society where residents live in their own country club. Employment provision includes only offices and research facilities. The town is structured in seven "villages," each focused on a different amenity: a lake, a golf course, etc. Buildings are clustered to leave generous open spaces. The architecture of the first village at Lake Anne departed from the suburban pattern by including tight groups of row houses. Its center, designed by W. Conklin, is a much admired miniature urban space (Plate 120).

Reston enjoyed the publicity advantages of a head start but Simon lacked experience and adequate financing and was soon forced to yield control to an oil company. As a result, the concept of high density "sinews" which Conklin proposed to tie together the nodal villages, has been abandoned and the architecture of the newer clusters has slipped in quality.

Columbia is situated on the fastest growing urban corridor of the region, halfway between Washington and Baltimore (Plate 121). Here the developer, J. Rouse, assembled 6,240 ha. of contiguous land. Planning began in 1962 with the target population set at 110,000, to be reached in fifteen years. Rouse is a sucessful developer of shopping centers and it seemed natural that his town should focus on a vast regional center aimed to capture the buying power of 250,000 customers (Plate 122). This disposition gave Columbia the prototypical image of a "city of efficient consumption," although this image shifted later when the town attracted substantial industry.

Rouse is determined to make a profit on his new town, and all design proposals had to be tested against an "economic model" to assure his creditors that they will get a good return on their money. However, the stated goals of Rouse are more lofty: Columbia is to become a "truly rational city" where anyone who works in one of the town's enterprises should find housing he can afford "from the janitor to the corporation president." In the long range, balance between job provision and the number of active population is envisaged, but without rigid staging as in the British new towns. Evidently Rouse considers his societal and economic goals to be compatible, although he never explained whether the societal goals are instrumental to the achievement of a good profit, or whether the profit is needed for the continued fostering of a better society.

The decision by General Electric to build a large appliance park in Columbia offering employment to many unskilled workers will soon test Rouse's determination to provide housing for all, against the reluctance of the present residents to accept such large-scale intrusion on their suburban idyll.[32]

Rouse favors a scientific planning process and he has

assembled a first-rate planning and management team assisted by a bevy of experts. Yet the physical plan shows no advance over the first generation British new towns and the densities are lower then in Stevenage. The town structure is hierarchical and nucleated—based on neighborhoods for 1,200 to 2,000 people forming villages of 6,000 to 10,000 residents (Plate 123). The planners proposed to provide public transport on its own right-of-way as in Runcorn—and surveys show that many people moved to Columbia in the hope that they would be able to live without needing *two* cars. But there is no economic way to provide adequate bus service with such low densities and, in fact, the population is totally dependent on the use of the private car.

Irvine, California, represents the third prototype of the American new town. In this case the catalyst in the decision for planning a new town was the need of a new campus for the University of California. The architect, W. Pereira, selected the site on the Irvine ranch, an enormous tract of undeveloped land in single ownership. The commitment of the university to build in the Irvine site obliged the corporation to engage in master planning for the entire area—instead of selling if off piecemeal.

The development of this ranch of 33,200 ha.—bigger than Washington D.C.—involved the mobilization of capital without parallel in the private sector. The present master plan for Irvine envisages a target population of half a million to 750,000 people and the provision of 134,000 industrial and 150,000 white-collar jobs (Plate 124). The first development sector between the university and the ocean covers 14,000 ha.—three times the size of Columbia, Md. Five minutes' drive from the campus a first town center was developed: Newport Center groups on a 250-ha. site shopping, medical, and financial facilities, professional offices, a golf course, and a hotel (Plate 125). This center includes the largest number of brokerage houses outside of a stock exchange area and embodies the "American dream of having Wall Street rise out of a country club." [33] An even larger town center will be developed on a triangular site formed by the intersection of three expressways.

Although the plan is composed of "villages" it is innovative in grouping schools, shops, institutions, and leisure facilities along an "environmental corridor" which, as a continuous green strip, provides an orienting element on the scale and speed of the automobile. Once a new town gains momentum, land for industry can bring in four times more then residential acreage and the Irvine Company is creating large industrial estates which already employ some 25,000 persons.

Reston, Columbia, and Irvine have characteristics that clearly set them apart from European new towns: low densities, the primacy accorded to the automobile, the emphasis on white-collar employment and on leisure facilities, and the high median income of the population.[34] A common problem of these privately developed new towns is how to transfer decision-making responsibility from the developer to the residents without endangering the goals and the timetable of the master plan. A suitable mechanism has been found in the Community Associations, with automatic membership of all residents. In Irvine, the goal of the association is "the preservation of property values." However, the conservatism of the first residents may block any intention to increase density by providing apartments for lower income groups; such a goal-conflict is already emerging in Columbia between the residents and the developers' intent to foster social mix and create a heterogeneous city.

Public attention focused on the new towns in the second half of the 1960s when projections of national population growth indicated that the decades until the end of the century may add 75 to 100 million more Americans to the present population,[35] and that most of this increase would tend to occur in the already overcrowded metropolitan areas. Favorable publicity about Reston, Columbia, and Irvine made the new towns appear as the panacea for the problems of urban growth. At the same time, the difficulties of the private developers with land assembly and financing demonstrated the need for federal assistance. This led first to an extension of the 1965 National Housing Act which offered loan guarantees for land acquisition for suburban subdivisions: in 1966 new communities were made eligible for these mortgages. But it was the 1968 Housing and Urban Development Act which marked the turning point in government involvement with new towns; in Title IV of this Act, Congress created loan guarantees to developers of new towns of up to fifty million dollars for a single project and established guidelines for new towns which must provide sufficient open space, balanced development, equal opportunity for minority groups and include low-cost housing. The authors of the Act distinguish four types of new towns: expanded towns, self-contained new towns, satellites, and "new-towns-in-town." This last term—a euphemism for large-scale urban renewal projects—was included as a palliative to big city mayors who voiced their concern that the new towns might divert federal aid from the central cities.

Also in 1968 the legislators of New York State went a step further by supporting Governor Rockefeller in the creation of an Urban Development Corporation equipped with the power to override local zoning and building codes and authorized to float one billion dollars in tax exempt bonds to finance its projects. Placed under the energetic leadership of Edward J. Logue, the UDC almost immediately announced its intention to create two new communities in upstate New York: Amherst, near Buffalo and Lysander, in the area of Syracuse. By 1970 the "New Communities for New York" report of the UDC proposed to channel no less then one-third of the anticipated population growth of the state into new communities.

Studies published between 1968–70 about the roots of the 1967 urban riots and pointing to the need for decongestion, influenced Congress in expanding its commitment to new towns by passing the Housing and Urban Development Act of 1970. This Act offers novel types of direct federal assistance to new communities and encourages social and technological experimentation. Title VII of the Act raised the ceiling on loan guarantees to new towns to a whopping 500 million dollars and extended the program to public agencies. Assuming that Congress allocates the necessary funds HUD is now in the position to assure the financial success of new community efforts, a provision so generous that G. Breckenfeld writing in *Fortune* described it as a "splendid chance for a new breed of promoter to get rich quick at the public's risk." In fact the provisions are sufficiently reassuring to attract to the field big corporations like General Electric, Ford, and the aerospace industry, while the formidable reputation of government red tape will prevent a rush of small speculators for the HUD bandwagon. Nevertheless, by 1971 hundreds of loan applications were reaching the Department of Housing and Urban Development and a trend emerged to start too many projects on too small a scale.

At the 1971 AIA Convention Lloyd Rodwin made the eminently sensible suggestion that the selection of new community projects for federal assistance should be made from the point of view of national growth objectives. New towns should not be individual showpieces but instruments of a larger strategy.[36] Rodwin also proposed the definition of goals for federal intervention and advocated the acceptance of public entities as developers and argued in favor of public ownership of urban land to harvest the economic values created by the new projects. However, given the American prejudice against planning as a form of regimentation, it will take another decade of public education to create social acceptance for such policies. In 1969 the National Committee on Urban Growth proposed the building of 100 new towns averaging 100,000 people and ten new towns of at least one million inhabitants. But, of 65 new communities presently in the planning stage, few approach the size of Columbia or Reston.[37] Yet there is already increasingly sharp criticism directed against the federal new town program: it is claimed that new towns sap the vitality of the center cities even more than the suburbs; that far from decongesting the center the new towns just "cream off" the best institutions, commerce, employment, and the better income groups—leaving the big city stuck with the hard-core unemployed and the multiple families.

The answer to such criticism is that the new towns will permit the testing of innovative ideas which eventually will help to restructure the center cities. But little has been achieved so far! Some new towns experiment with novel means of rapid transit: Fairlane—planned by the Ford Motor Company—will have a rail link to Detroit and to the airport; Park Forest South—planned for 110,000 mixed-income people—will be served by internal rapid transit with a link to the Chicago Loop; Flower Mound, located between Dallas and Fort Worth, will have the giant international airport as its employment base. Audubon, N.Y.[38] is based on the new

Amherst campus of the State University with its 26,000 students and 13,000 employees, yet it will only accomodate 27,500 people, with a low density like at Reston. With its 800 ha. and 9,000 dwelling units, it is on a "laboratory scale" toward larger ventures by the New York State UDC (Plates 126, 127).

Undoubtably more new towns focused on universities and on research will be proposed. One of the most interesting developments is the possible rise of Black New Towns, communities developed by black entrepreneurs or nonprofit corporations to open jobs and housing to blacks, while remaining open to all. The idea of Black New Towns evolved from the desire of militant blacks to leave the ghetto but refusing to be absorbed into a minority role in the suburbs.[39]

Soul City, North Carolina, is promoted by Floyd Mc Kissick of the Congress of Racial Equality. It will be a self-contained new town sixty-five km. north of Durham. Two other black new towns await HUD approval, one in Alabama another in South Carolina. Such new towns with a black power structure will give a focus to black enterprise as an alternative to reluctant integration into the white-dominated suburbs; they offer the more dynamic elements of the black community a choice to go their own way and run their own life.

Just how much all these new towns will accomplish is difficult to assess. In 1972 Lloyd Rodwin attempted some educated crystal-ball gazing and predicted the completion of about forty American new towns before the end of the century. Since Mr. Rodwin opposes the proliferation of small new communities, his forecast was meant to be normative and it seems more likely that twice his number will be built, although few will be innovative showpieces. Some independent new towns may be built to revitalize lagging regions but it is more likely that such towns will be of the type of our resort-and-special-communities with planned populations up to 100,000. The new towns within the metropolitan areas will not significantly relieve the center cities: they might however achieve the restructuring of the disorderly land-use tissue of the large conurbations. In this their role will be comparable to the objective given to the *villes nouvelles* of the Paris region.

6 CONCLUSIONS

Having surveyed past and present new town building we may now venture some "surprise-free" predictions concerning the new communities likely to be built up until the end of this century. Although the decade 1950–1960 saw the rise of three important new capital cities, such a rate can hardly be sustained. Yet some nations which recently acquired independence will undoubtedly decide to build new capitals that are likely to have a double role as administrative centers and as economic growth poles of a development region.

In the sparsely settled areas of Asiatic Russia, Brazil, Canada, Australia, etc., increased efforts will be made at internal colonization, requiring both new industrial towns and service centers for agricultural regions.

New technology harnessing the energy of the ocean tides, capturing solar energy, and more economically exploiting nuclear fission will permit the colonization of the tundra, the reconquest of the Sahara and of other desert regions by extensive irrigation and perhaps even underwater farming on the continental shelf. The exploitation of underwater coal and oil fields will lead to new forms of industrial towns—artificial islands and floating communities—as proposed by the Japanese "Metabolist" group of architects for Tokyo Bay. Competition for mineral resources will lead to the colonization of both the Arctic regions and of the Antarctic by building towns with completely controlled microclimate within closed pyramidal or spherical superstructures—recalling the visionary ideas of Buckminster Fuller. Such concepts already receive serious attention in schools of architecture of the Soviet Union.

The traditional type of industrial town will of course account for the largest number of new foundations in developing countries. The emerging economic equilibrium between advanced countries and the so-called Third World will lead to a division of labor with the advanced countries gradually yielding the polluting heavy industries and crude technology to the developing countries in favor of concentrating more exclusively on manufacturing that requires sophisticated technology and highly skilled labor (such as electronics, optics, pharmaceutical, chemistry, computers and other miniaturized instruments). Some developing countries will also have to face the problem created by the gigantism of their principal cities and build "parallel cities" in the 1 to 3 million range—as the only rational way to avoid the collapse of all municipal services.

In advanced countries, decongestion of the large conurbations will remain the dominant problem, and one may predict the creation of numerous satellites and balanced new towns in the 100,000 to 300,000 range, as well as the development of extended towns on the English or French model—up to half a million people in size. There will be growing discrepancy between the deteriorating central cities and the new environment of these outlying communities.

The wealth and abundant free time of the emerging post-industrial societies will foster the creation of numerous "specialized communities" in the 50,000 to 100,000 people range. These will be "parasitic" in the Marxist sense—lacking any productive employment base. In addition to retirement communities and large high-density resort towns—such as the Grande Motte near Montpellier (France)—one might predict the rise of some frankly hedonistic communities of nudists, homosexuals, and so forth—as well as their counterpart—comtemplative, monastic, and utopian communes such as Auroville, presently built near Madras for 50,000 followers of the guru Sri Aurobindo. Such leisure- and/or contemplation-oriented communes will be financed by private groups, but for more conventional new towns the trend is clearly toward an increasing regulatory role of the government and toward public involvement in land assembly and financing even in capitalist democracies.

Within the next twenty-five years several hundred new towns will be founded—designed to contain twenty to thirty million people. Although this figure might seem large, it represents only two to five percent of the total need of new housing, jobs and services that will be required to accommodate the one billion additional people that will crowd the world's urban areas, according to projections of demographic growth and the rate of world urbanization. In view of the tremendous pressures that these figures imply for existing towns, the question is often raised whether the creation of new towns is worth the effort. Granted that the new towns in the long run will return to the nation the capital advanced for their development—or so the argument runs—but new town building monopolizes the budget available for urban investment; and in a sense the minority of new town residents are unduly privileged and subsidized by the larger community. Would the money not be better spent by giving priority to the renewal of existing cities?

The answer is, of course, that money invested in the new towns is supposed to bring a better return—yield more housing, jobs, amenities—than the same sum invested in town renewal. The creation of new towns also bypasses the problem of relocation and even the problems of land assembly are less cumbersome than in the built-up areas. Secondly, it is not possible to tackle the problems of the existing towns without stabilizing their population at present densities—by siphoning off at least some of the "overspill" population to new towns. Such relief may also be the only way to save the historical environment of old towns from destruction by attempting to adapt the old core to serve the central functions of an ever larger metropolitan area.

The problem still remains how to make the building of new towns more socially acceptable. In this, one may quote Hugh Wilson—the designer of Cumbernauld—who stated that the effort is only justifiable if "the new towns are considered as laboratories in which ideas for the restructuration of existing cities are elaborated." There can be no question that the experience is transferable: valid concepts developed in new towns have already proved their usefulness in application to existing cities—not the least of these gains is the concept of the "new-towns-in-town" or very large-scale comprehensive renewal projects, benefiting to some extent from the same scale economies as the construction of a new town. To further the experimental role of new towns it will be essential to better coordinate their building with other programs of national scope, such as regional development or the building of new university and research centers. This goal may seem self evident, yet negative examples abound. For example in Great Britain as many new universities have been built since the war as there are new towns, yet there is not a single case where the building of a new town and of a new university have been coordinated. It is also interesting to reflect on the possibility of creating demonstration new towns in connection with such unique events as Olympic Games or World's Fairs. The recent record of such events proves that they can mobilize an astonishing amount of public investment which often leaves very substantial permanent equipment to the host town. While even the modest Seattle Fair bequeathed the town an opera house and a monorail—the 1970 Osaka Fair resulted in three billion dollars worth of public improvements, including the new town of Senri; and the 1972 Munich Olympics, which lasted only a few days, benefited the town with vast sports and recreation facilities and a model housing estate for 18,000 people.

The United States has passed up a unique chance in not opting to build a demonstration new town to celebrate the 1976 bicentennials; such a town could have offered an experimental urban form, innovative equipment, and an ecologically sane and satisfying urban way of living. New towns have a taste-forming educational function demonstrating alternate modes of urban living. This is vital since people's aspirations are largely formed by the familiar. It seems particularly urgent to demonstrate alternatives to the land-wasting garden suburb which has such popular appeal in English-speaking countries (see note 19 Chapter 5). Here, university research may play an important role: the model of a high-density new town was developed by the Graduate School of Design at Harvard University (Plate 128), with costs estimated against a popular spread-out development of the same population. It could be proved that the high density model was significantly cheaper to build, to run and to live in. Yet only by building such a town full-scale can people be convinced that the model will not only be cheaper but also offer a superior living environment. As Von Hertzen puts it: "people cannot be enlightened by paper plans, they need a living model to judge." Given the menacing increase in congestion, pollution, overurbanization, and sprawl—all pointing to continued worldwide deterioration of the urban environment—the voluntarist policy of creating new towns is one way to prove that "trend is not destiny" (Albert Mayer) and to ensure future generations of a total urban environment that may not be better—but should be no worse—than the world we have inherited.

THE PLATES

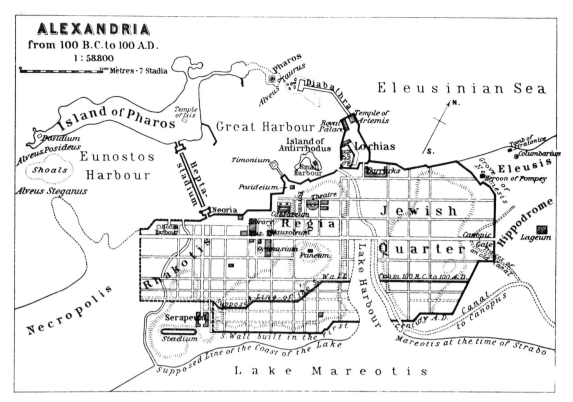

1 Reconstructed plan of Alexandria, capital of Ptolemaic Egypt,
100 B.C.–100 A.D., after Wagner and Debes. Perimeter wall is
Roman.

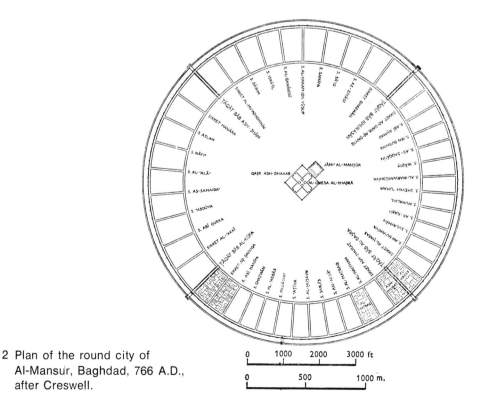

2 Plan of the round city of
Al-Mansūr, Baghdad, 766 A.D.,
after Creswell.

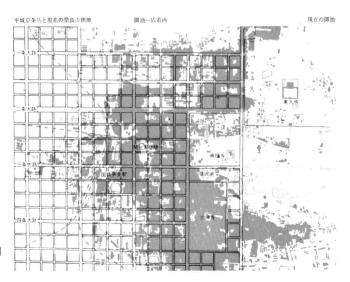

3 Plan of Changan, capital of the T'ang dynasty.

4 Plan of Heijokyo (modern Nara), 710 A.D., superimposed on modern built-up area.

5 (*left*) Plan of Heiankyo,
794 A.D. (modern Kyoto):
topographic situation.

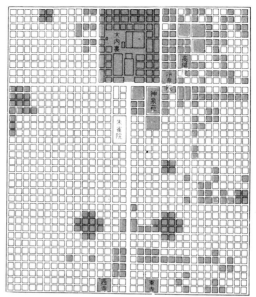

6 Schematic plan of Heiankyo.

7 Mandalay, Burma. 1930
plan of the new town
founded in 1857.

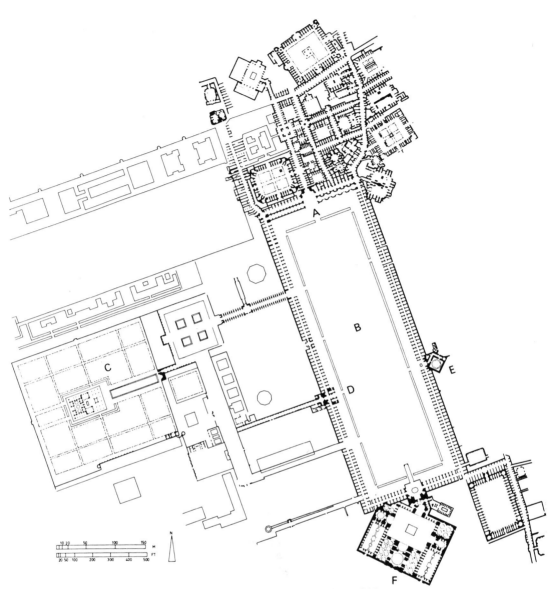

A

B

C

D

E

F

8 Plan of civic center, Isfahan, Persia, as completed in 1628.

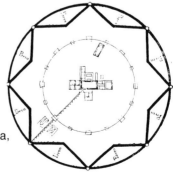

9 Plan of an ideal city, Sforzinda,
by Filarete, 1464.

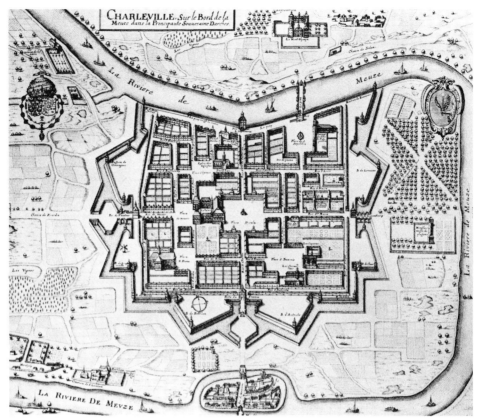

10 Plan of Charleville, France, 1656.

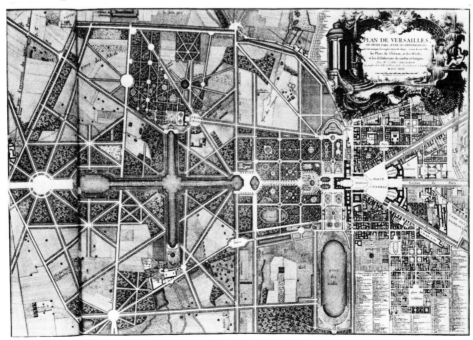

11 Plan of Versailles, 1746.

12 Plans of St. Petersburg

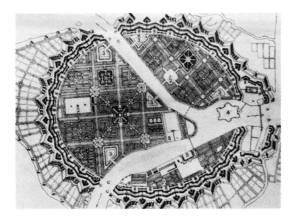

a. Plan of Leblond, 1717.

b. Plan engraved by I. B.
Homann, 1718.

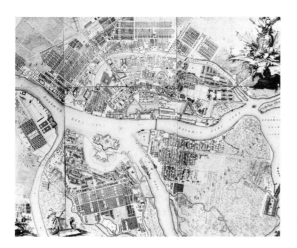

c. Plan engraved by N. I.
Machajev, 1753.

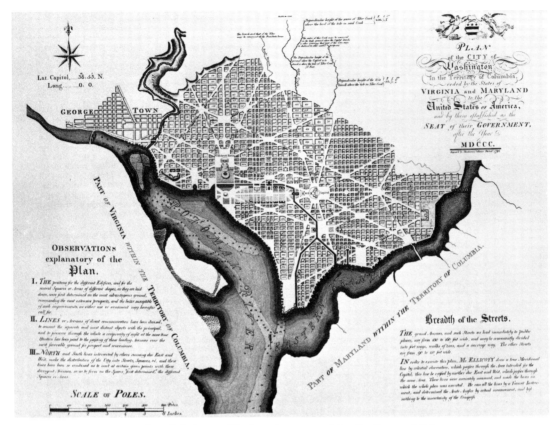

13 Plan for Washington, D.C., slightly modified and engraved by Endicott, 1792.

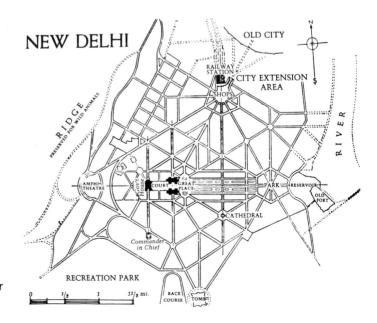

14 Plan of New Delhi by Sir Edwin Lutyens, 1911.

15 Plan of Canberra by Walter
Burley Griffin, 1911.

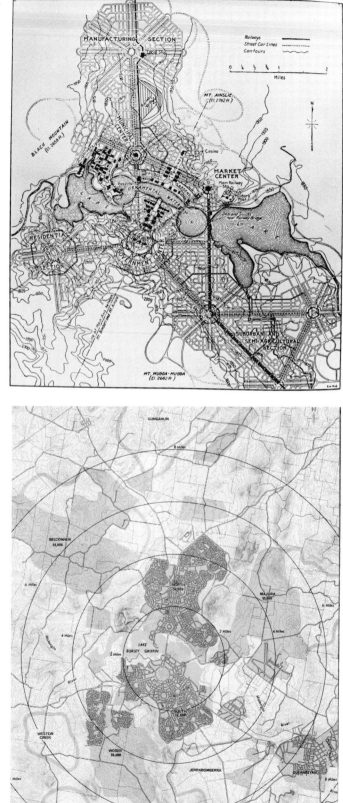

16 Plan of Canberra, Australia,
1972. Built-up area, and
capacity of new suburbs.

17 Canberra: Master Plan of center area, 1970.

1 War memorial and parade
3 City center
6 Executive offices
13 Parliamentary zone
15 Conference zone
16 Cultural zone

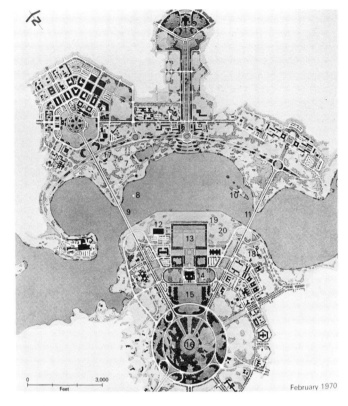

February 1970

18 Canberra: aerial views of center area

a. City center, 1970.

b. City area looking south,
1972.

19 Aerial view
   of La Plata,
   Argentina,
   founded
   1883.

20 Belo-
   Horizonte,
   Brazil. 1940
   plan of the
   new town
   founded in
   1897.

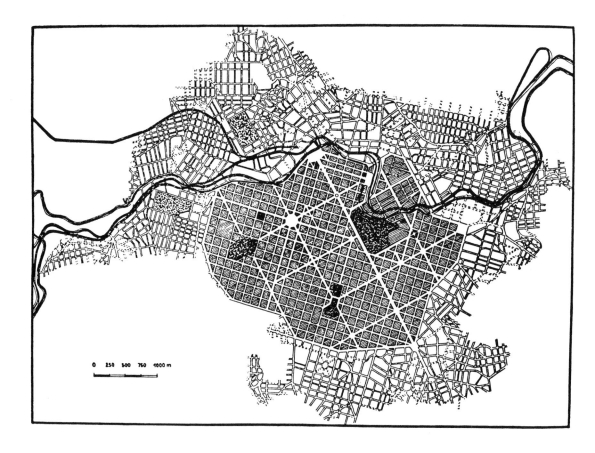

0   250   500   750   1000 m

21 Plans of Brasilia

a. Central area or formal city,
   1971.

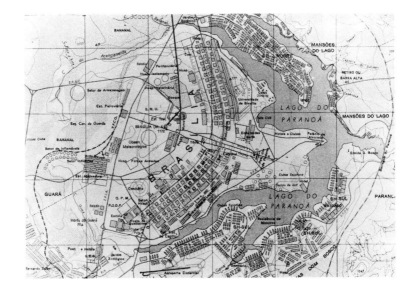

b. Regional setting with
   satellite towns, 1969.

22 Aerial views
of Brasilia,
1970.

a. Looking east along monumental axis.

b. Looking south along residential axis.

Unidades urbanas do projeto M. M. M. Roberto

23 Brasilia, alternate project by
the Roberto Brothers: one of
the cellular urban units.

24 Chandigarh, India, original
Master Plan by Albert Mayer,
1950.

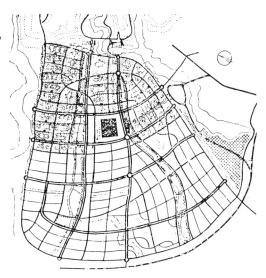

25 Chandigarh: the Le Corbusier
plan.
Actual layout, 1970.

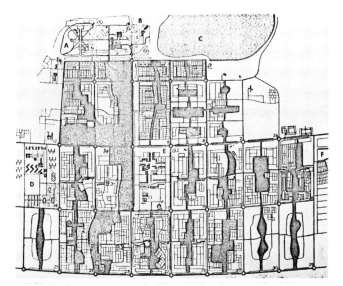

26 Chandigarh, Capitol area:
Secretariat.

27 Islamabad,
Pakistan,
proposed
dynamic growth
pattern by C.
Doxiades
Associates,
1962.

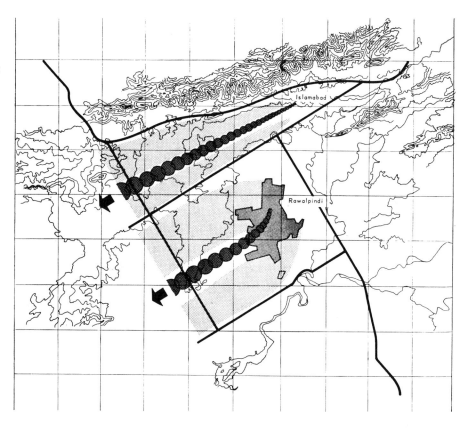

28 Islamabad,
Pakistan:
Master Plan of
metropolitan
area by C.
Doxiades
Associates,
1960.

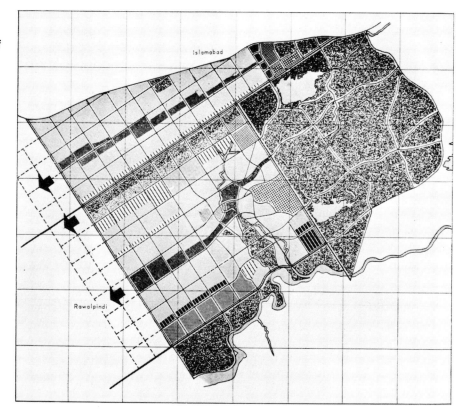

29 Islamabad, model photographs of government area and two residential sectors, 1962.

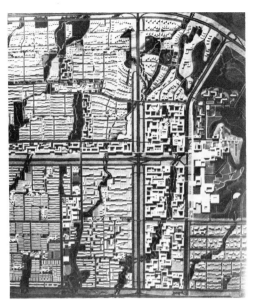

30 Islamabad, plan of a typical community, Class V, by Doxiades, 1962.

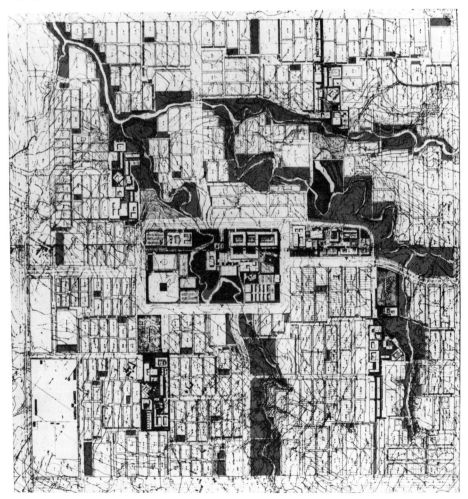

31 Master Plan of Lelystad,
  Ijselmeerpolder, S.
  Netherlands, by C. Van
  Eesteren, submitted to Dutch
  Government in 1964.

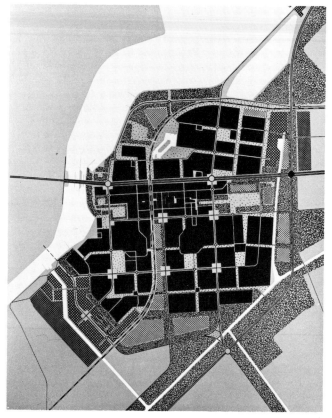

32 Lelystad, view of town center,
  1971.

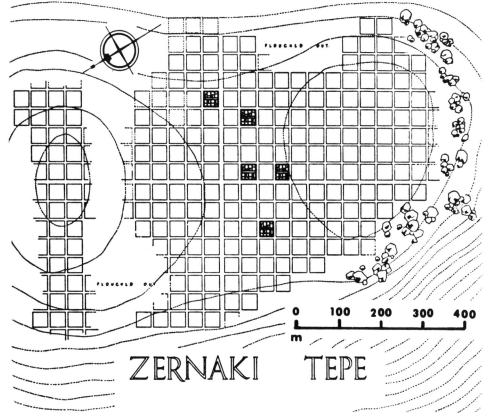

FLOUGHED OUT.

FLOUGHED OUT

0   100   200   300   400

m

ZERNAKI TEPE

33 Plan of Zernaki Tepe, eighth century B.C.

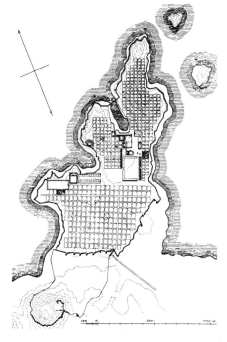

34 Plan of Miletus, 479 B.C.

35 (Thamagudi), Timgad, aerial view of Roman colony founded 100 B.C.

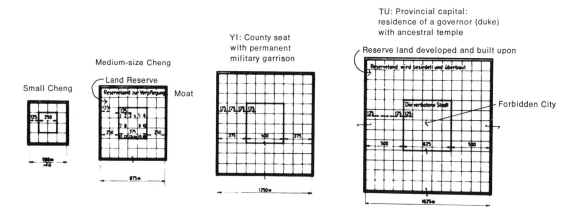

Small Cheng

Medium-size Cheng

Land Reserve
Reserveland zur Verpflegung
Moat

YI: County seat
with permanent
military garrison

TU: Provincial capital:
residence of a governor (duke)
with ancestral temple

Reserve land developed and built upon
Reserveland wird besiedelt und überbaut

Die verbotene Stadt
Forbidden City

36 Feudal hierarchy of Chinese settlements. Chou Dynasty, 1122–256 B.C.

37 Monastery plan of St. Gall, early ninth century.

38 Bern, aerial view of town foundation in 1191 A.D.

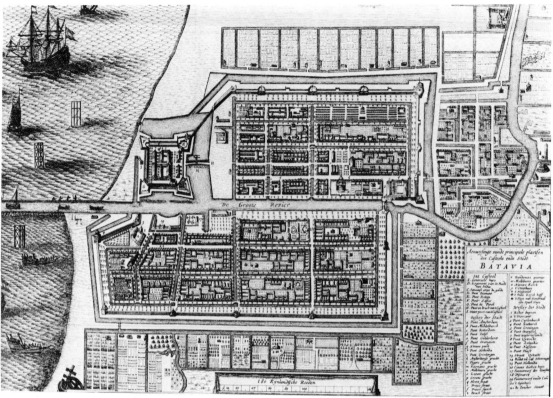

39 Plan of Batavia (Jakarta), 1619.

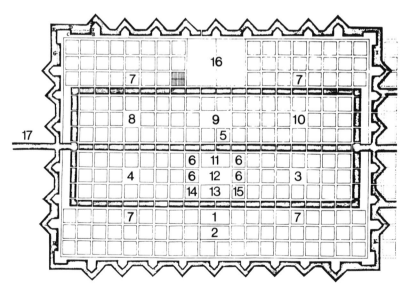

1 College
2 Poorhouse
3 Building materials (stone) market
4 Haymarket
5 Meat market
6 Lots reserved for public buildings
7 Church
8 Corn market
9 Principal market square
10 Cattle market
11 Main church
12 Exchange
13 City hall
14 Weights and measures department
15 Fabric hall
16 Place and court
17 Quay (for unloading barges)

40 Simon Stevin, ideal plan for new town, 1649.

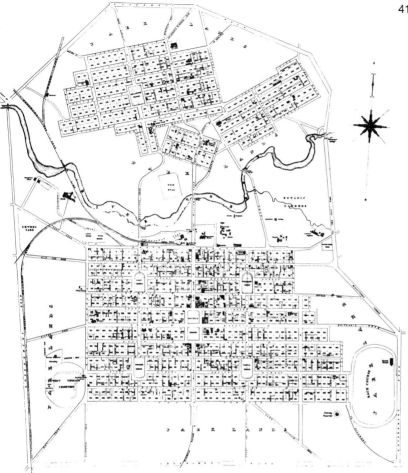

41 Plan of Adelaide and
North Adelaide,
Australia, as drawn by
P. F. Sinnett, 1881.

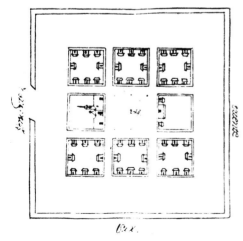

42 Standard 3 × 3 block,
Hispanoamerican
colonial town plan.

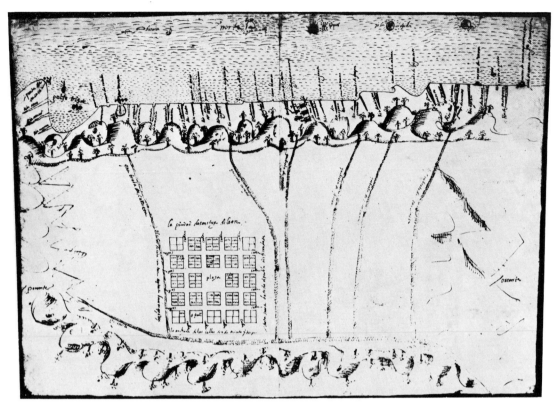

43 Sixteenth-century plan of Caracas, founded 1567.

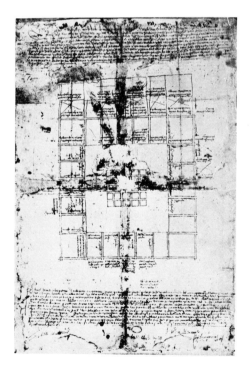

44 Plans of Mendoza, Argentina
a. Town surrounded by farm
   plots, 1561.

b. The town plat, 1562; note
   monasteries in the four
   corners.

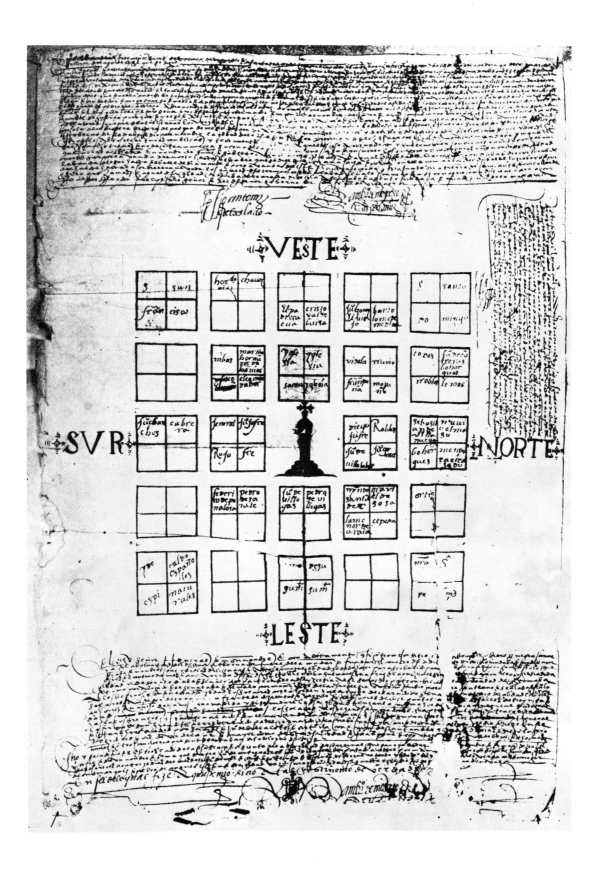

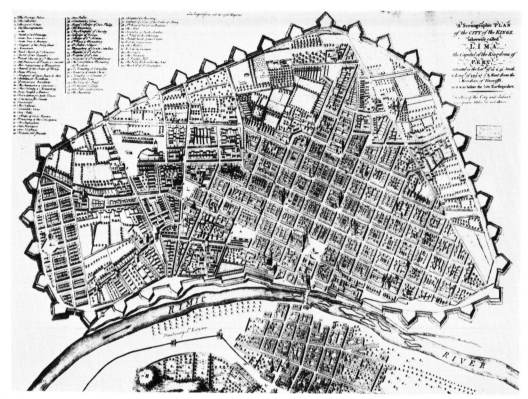

45 Plan of Lima, Peru, 1683.

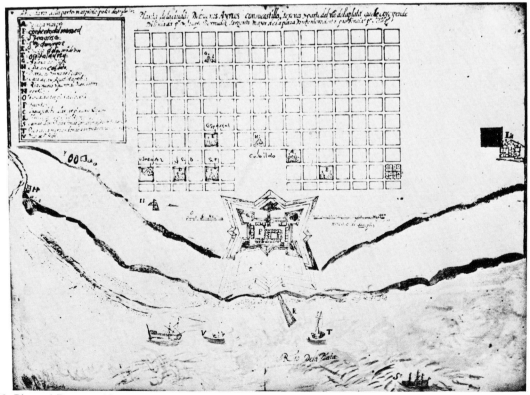

46 Plan of Buenos Aires, rendering, 1708.

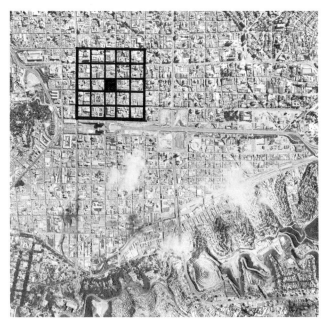

47 Aerial view of Caracas with outline of original traza over present structure.

48 Aerial view of Santa Fe de Granada, Spain, 1492.

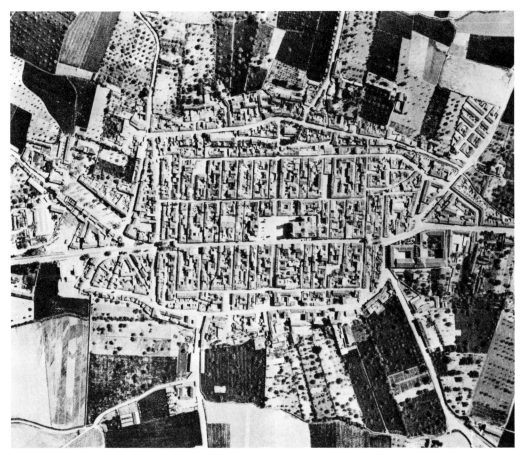

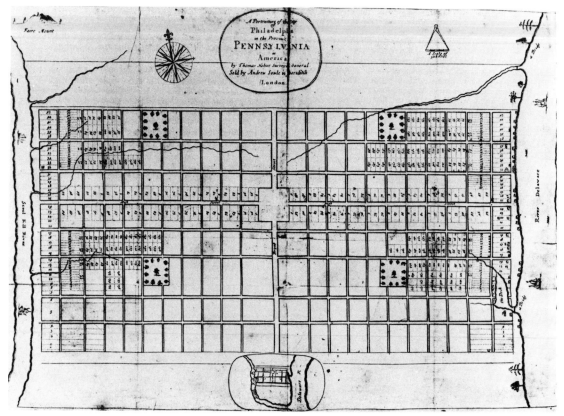

49 William Penn's plan for Philadelphia, 1682, drawn by Thomas Holme.

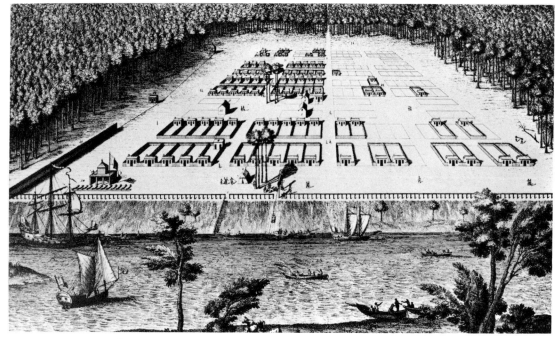

50a View of Savannah, Georgia,
1739.

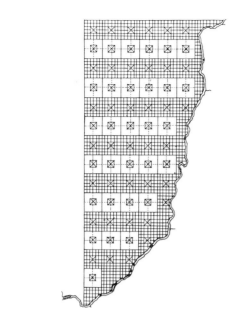

50b 1785 land ordinance as applied to first townships in Ohio.

51 Aerial view of Grammichele, Sicily, founded in 1693.

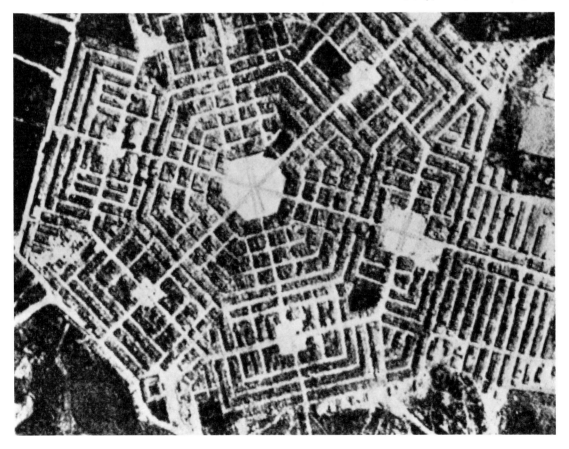

52 Beer Sheba, Israel, general
plan 1964.

Wohngebiet
Residential area
Haupt- und
Nebenzentren
Main and sub-centres
Industrie / Industry
Handwerk, Gewerbe
Crafts and small
industries
Sport / Sports
Krankenhaus
Hospital

Friedhof / Cemetery

Hauptstraße, geplant
Main road, projected
Nebenstraße, geplant
Secondary road,
projected
Autobusstation
Central bus station
Eisenbahn, geplant
Railway, projected
Bahnhof, geplant
Railway station,
projected

1 Altstadt / Old town
V Mustersiedlung
Model neigh-
bourhood
2 Stadtverwaltung
Town administra-
tion
3 Krankenhaus
Hospital
4 Negev Arid
Zone Research
Institute
5 Stadthalle
Community centre
6 Distriktsver-
waltung
District
administration
7 Großmarkthalle
Market hall
8 Stadion / Stadium

Ausgrabungsgebiet
Excavation zone

Stadtgrenze
Municipal boundary

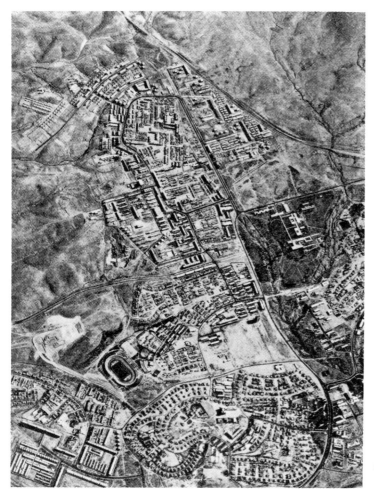

53 Beer Sheba, Israel,
aerial view 1968.

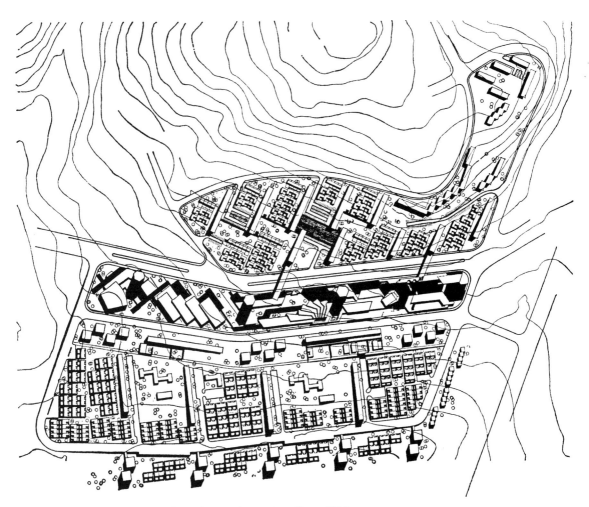

54 Karmiel, Israel, plan of first phase of construction, 1964.

55 Plan of Hotep Sesostris, 1890
B.C. Larger houses at top
were apparently for overseers.

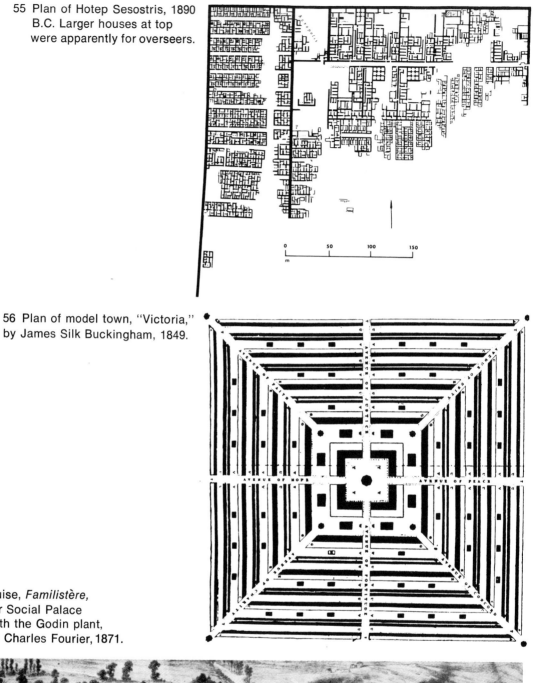

56 Plan of model town, "Victoria,"
by James Silk Buckingham, 1849.

AVENUE OF HOPE   AVENUE OF PEACE

57 Guise, *Familistère,*
for Social Palace
with the Godin plant,
by Charles Fourier, 1871.

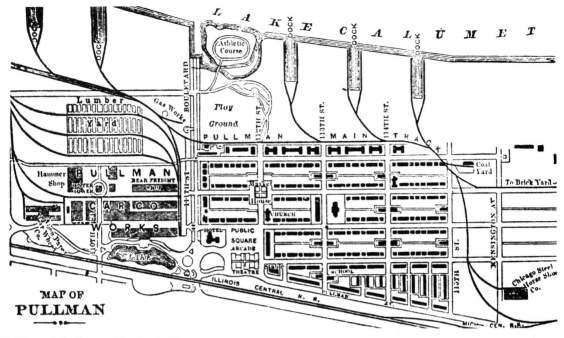

58 Plan of Pullman, Illinois, 1885.

59 Plan of Gary, Indiana, 1907.

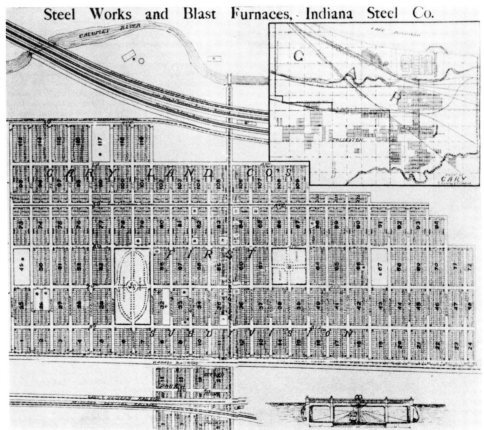

60 Diagram of Soviet industrial town after Shkvarikov, 1966.

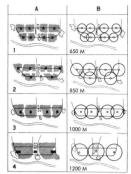

61 Aerial views of
   Dunaujvaros, Hungary.
   Planned in 1950.

a. View southwest
   toward steel mill.

b. View southeast with
   Danube.

62 Salgotarjan, Hungary, view of town center,
1973.

63 Wolfsburg, Germany, general plan, 1938.

STADT WOLFSBURG – PLANUNGSLEITBILD 1972

64 Wolfsburg, Germany, pilot
plan of 1972.

65 Wolfsburg, main street and pre-W.W.II Area.

65a Wolfsburg, Dermerode
sector, view toward center.

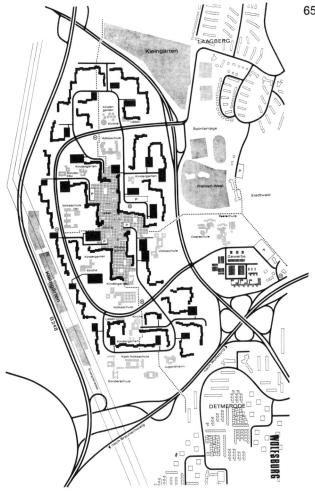

65b Wolfsburg, Plan of
Westhagen sector, 1968.
15,000 persons; gross
density 117 persons per ha.

65c Wolfsburg, cultural center by
Alvar Aalto 1970.

66 Ciudad Guayana, Venezuela,
the national steel works, 1971.

67 Ciudad Guayana, the Guri
dam and artificial lake
created by damming the
Caroní River.

68 Ciudad
Guayana,
General Plan

a. Original
   1971.

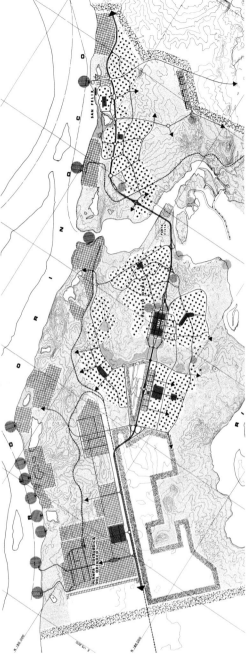

b. For
   300,000
   inhabi-
   tants.

69 Ciudad Guayana, view west toward steel mill, 1968.

70 Ciudad Guayana, the center. Alta Vista, 1969.

71 Ciudad Guayana, view towards east and south, Felix Center, 1970.

72 Ciudad Guayana, view towards NE, Porto Ordaz Center, 1968.

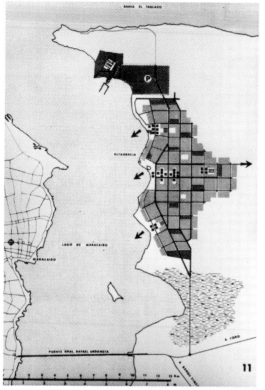

73 El Tablazo, Venezuela,
   schematic plan, 1968.

74 El Tablazo, photo of model of
   town.

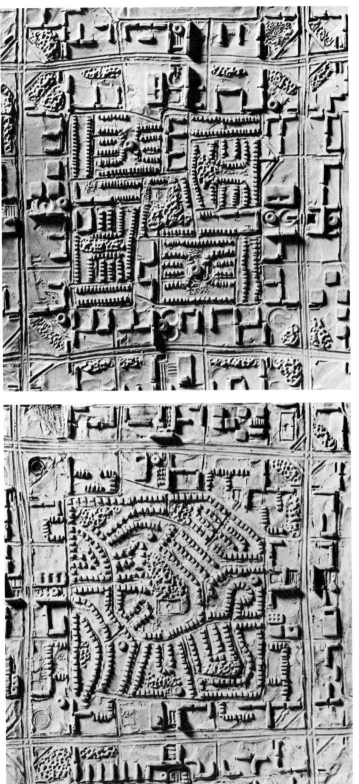

75a & b El Tablazo, two photos
of model illustrating
spatial form of a sector.

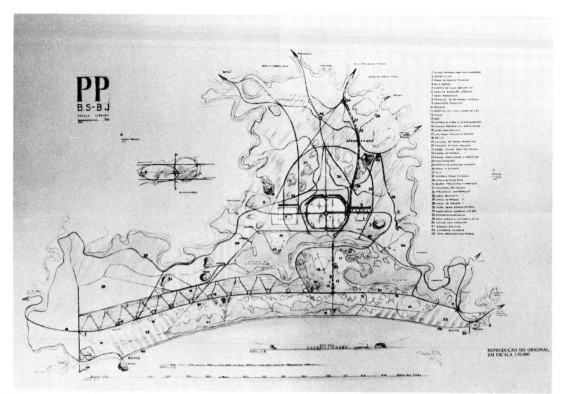

76 Plan of Jacaparagua, Brazil,
sketch by Lucio Costa, 1970.
Parallel city of Rio de Janeiro.

1 Metropolitan center (regional CBD)
2 Civic center (government)
7, 21, 22 Lagunes, nature reserves
12 Museum
19 Medium-high-density apartment buildings
20 Low-density individual homes
30 Low-income (workers') residential area
31 Nontoxic industries
37 Rapid-transit line to Rio (metro)
39 Agricultural area
43 Permanent exhibition area

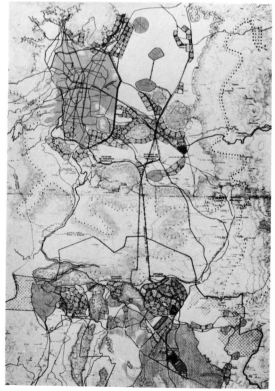

77 Mexico City and Ciudad
Paralela. Procicsa proposal
of 1970.

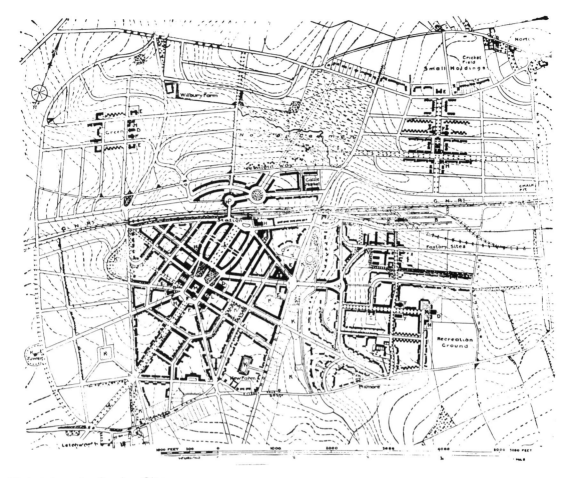

78 Letchworth, Garden City,
1903.

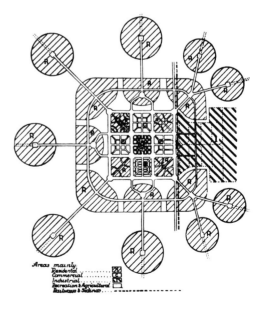

79 Raymond Unwin, town with
satellites, 1922.

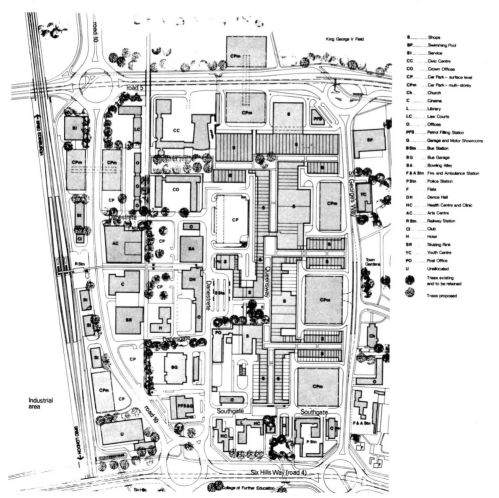

80 Ernst Gloeden, nuclear towns, 1923.

Electric rapid transit lines ———
Other railroads − − − −

81 Stevenage, England, plan of town center, 1962. First completely pedestrian center.

EL. SCHNELL-B
BAHNEN ALS
FLACH-HOCH-
UNTERGRUND-
V EINSCHNITT-
BAHNEN.

SCHUL-
BEZIRK

Maßstab 1 : 50 000

S ——— Shops
SP —— Swimming Pool
SI ——— Service
CC —— Civic Centre
CO —— Crown Offices
CP —— Car Park – surface level
CPm —— Car Park – multi-storey
Ch —— Church
C ——— Cinema
L ——— Library
LC —— Law Courts
O ——— Offices
PFS —— Petrol Filling Station
G ——— Garage and Motor Showrooms
B Stn —— Bus Station
BG —— Bus Garage
BA —— Bowling Alley
F & A Stn —— Fire and Ambulance Station
P Stn —— Police Station
F ——— Flats
DH —— Dance Hall
HC —— Health Centre and Clinic
AC —— Arts Centre
R Stn —— Railway Station
Cl ——— Club
H ——— Hotel
SR —— Skating Rink
YC —— Youth Centre
PO —— Post Office
U ——— Unallocated
● Trees existing and to be retained
Trees proposed

King George V Field

road 10
road 5
road 10

Danestrete
Queensway
St Georges Way
Danestrete
Danesgate
Southgate
Southgate

Industrial area

Town Gardens

Six Hills Way (road 4)
Six Hills
College of Further Education

82 Aerial view of Stevenage Center 1966.

83 Harlow, England, "Casbah" housing group. M. Neylan, architect, 1966.

84 Harlow, industry and Mark Hall neighborhoods.

85 Harlow, Great Parndon Area.

86 Hook, town pedestrian
system, 1961.

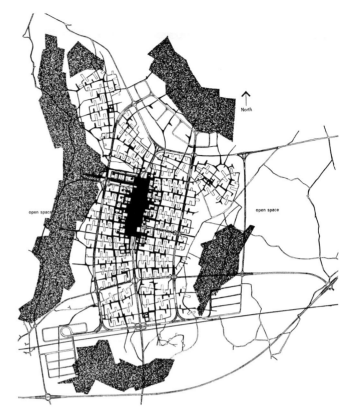

87 Hook, master road plan, 1961.

88 Cumbernauld, Scotland, 1968, aerial view.

89 Cumbernauld, 1968, city center in construction.

90 Cumbernauld, schematic land-use plan, 1958.

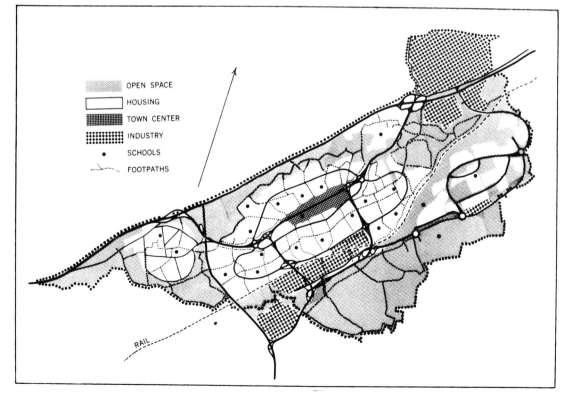

OPEN SPACE

HOUSING

TOWN CENTER

INDUSTRY

SCHOOLS

FOOTPATHS

RAIL

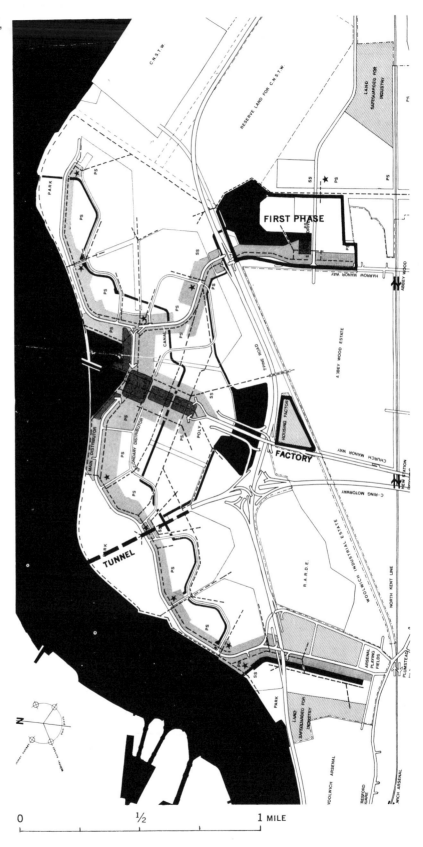

91 Thamesmead, England,
Master Plan.

92 Model of Thamesmead development, 1969.

93 Thamesmead, Phase I, 1972.

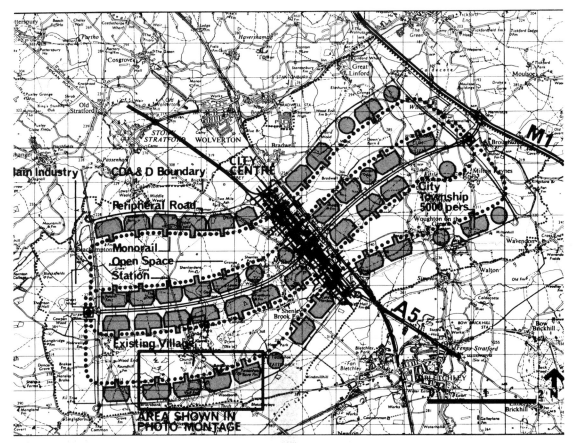

94 Milton
Keynes,
England,
first
proposal by
architect
F. B. Pooley,
1964.

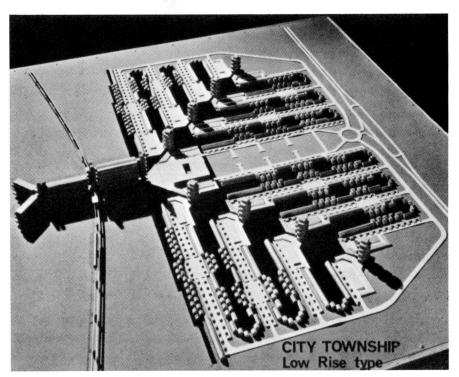

95 Milton
Keynes,
Pooley plan:
model of
township,
1964.

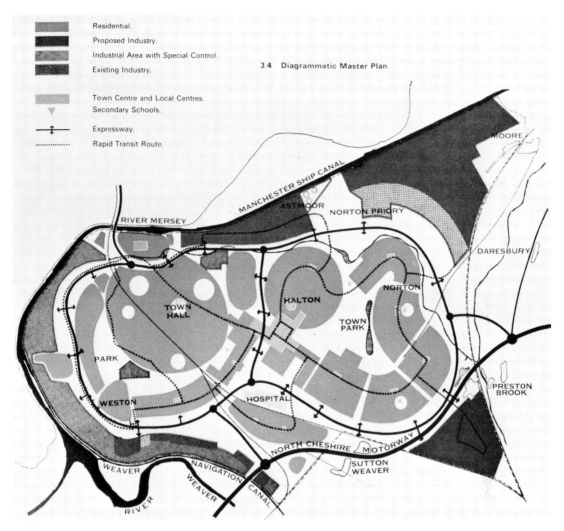

Residential.
Proposed Industry.
Industrial Area with Special Control.
Existing Industry.

Town Centre and Local Centres.
Secondary Schools.
Expressway.
Rapid Transit Route.

3.4   Diagrammatic Master Plan.

96 Runcorn, England, Arthur
    Ling and Associates,
    diagrammatic Master Plan,
    1967.

97 Runcorn, diagrammatic
    community structure, 1967.

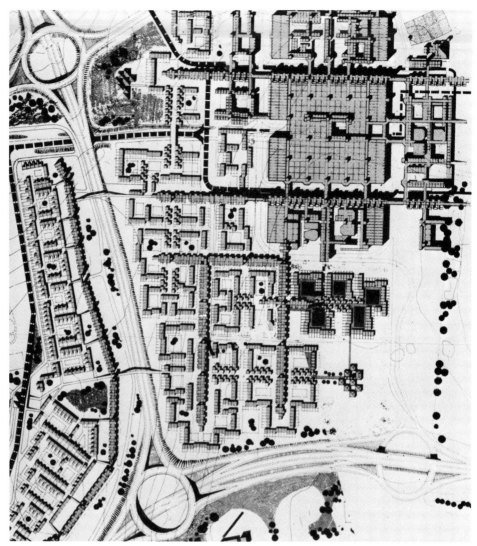

98 Runcorn, Urban Center Plan, 1967.

99 Runcorn, Model of first stage of Urban Center, 1967.

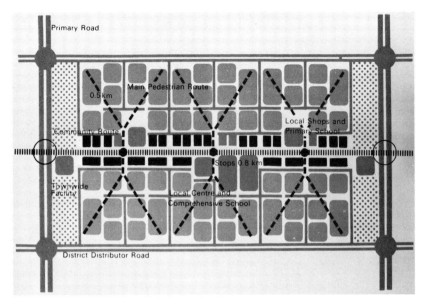

100 Irvine, Scotland, diagrammatic community
structure, 1970.

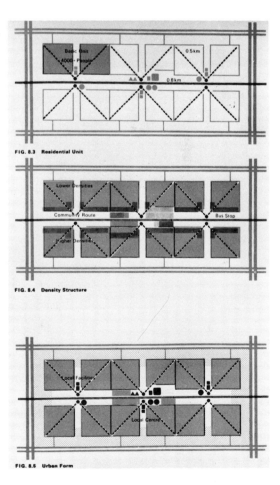

FIG. 8.3 Residential Unit

FIG. 8.4 Density Structure

FIG. 8.5 Urban Form

101 Irvine, Scotland, diagrams of residential
unit, density, urban form, 1970.

102 Milton Keynes, strategic plan by Llewelyn-Davis and Partners, 1970.

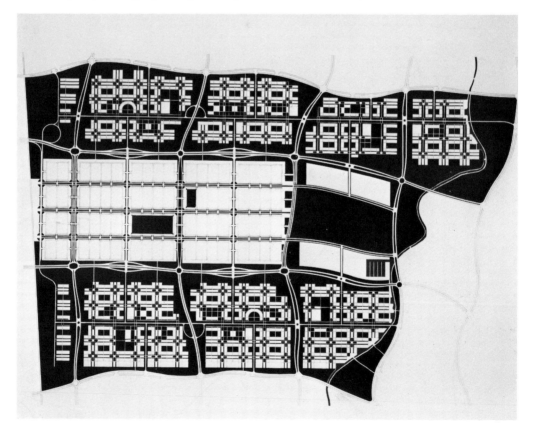

103 Milton Keynes, Central Milton Keynes by Llewelyn-Davis and Partners, 1970.

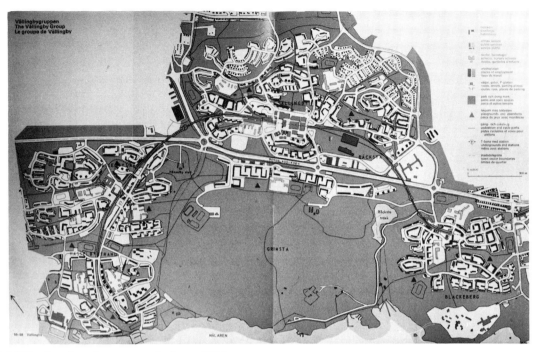

104 Vällingby, Sweden, general plans, 1954.

105 Vällingby, aerial view of center, 1970.

106 Aerial photo of
satellite, Täby,
Sweden, 1972.

107 Plan of Tapiola,
Finland, 1953.

108 Tapiola, 1970, aerial view.

109 Tapiola, view of town center, architect Aarne Ervi, 1970.

110 Senri, Japan, New Town, 1970.

111 Senri, 1970.

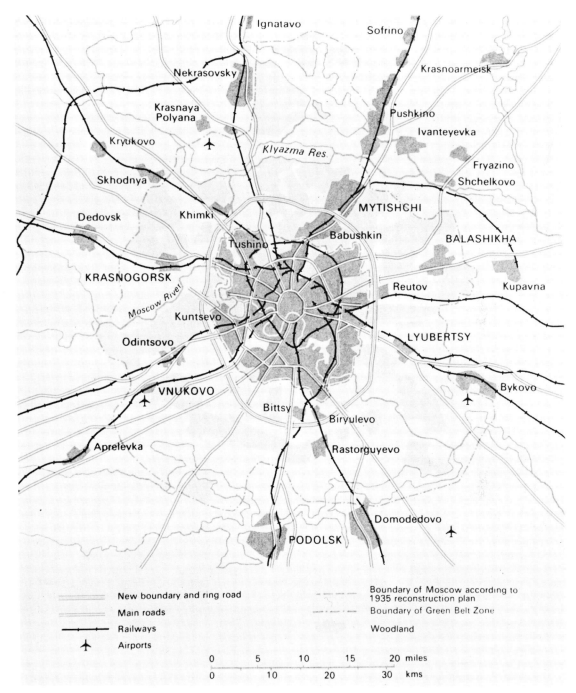

Ignatavo

Sofrino

Nekrasovsky

Krasnoarmeisk

Krasnaya
Polyana

Pushkino

Kryukovo

Ivanteyevka

Klyazma Res.

Fryazino

Skhodnya

Shchelkovo

Dedovsk

Khimki

Tushino

Babushkin

MYTISHCHI

BALASHIKHA

KRASNOGORSK

Moscow River

Kuntsevo

Reutov

Kupavna

Odintsovo

LYUBERTSY

VNUKOVO

Bittsy

Bykovo

Biryulevo

Aprelevka

Rastorguyevo

Domodedovo

PODOLSK

	New boundary and ring road		Boundary of Moscow according to 1935 reconstruction plan
	Main roads		Boundary of Green Belt Zone
	Railways		Woodland
	Airports		

| 0 | 5 | 10 | 15 | 20 miles |
| 0 | 10 | 20 | | 30 kms |

112 Moscow, Russia, the city and the region, 1960.

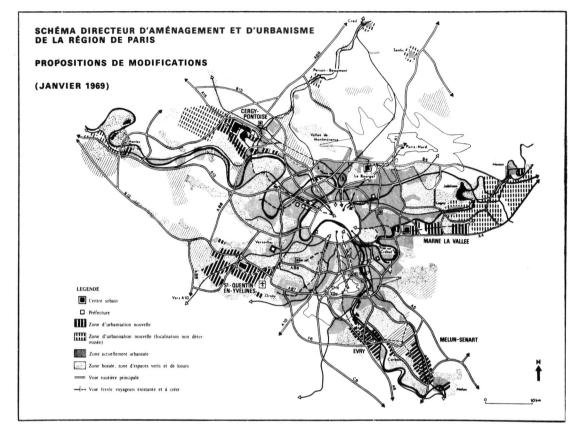

113 Paris Regional Master Plan, 1969, locating five satellite towns.

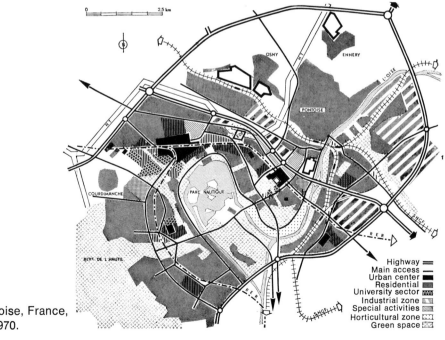

Highway
Main access
Urban center
Residential
University sector
Industrial zone
Special activities
Horticultural zone
Green space

114 Cergy-Pontoise, France,
    site plan, 1970.

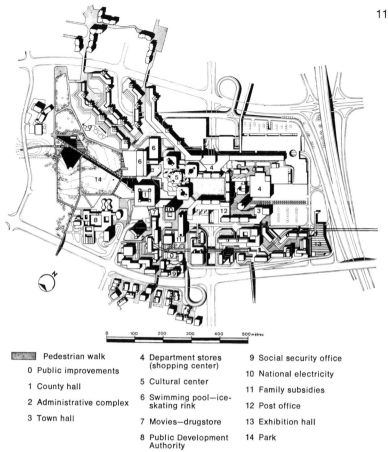

115 Cergy, plan
of the
center,
1972.

░░ Pedestrian walk	

0 Public improvements

1 County hall

2 Administrative complex

3 Town hall

4 Department stores (shopping center)

5 Cultural center

6 Swimming pool—ice-skating rink

7 Movies—drugstore

8 Public Development Authority

9 Social security office

10 National electricity

11 Family subsidies

12 Post office

13 Exhibition hall

14 Park

116 Cergy, the "Prefecture," 1972.

117 Cergy, the
center, 1972.

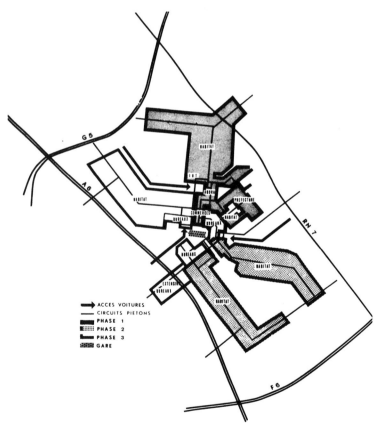

118 Site plan of Evry,
New Town,
France, 1972.

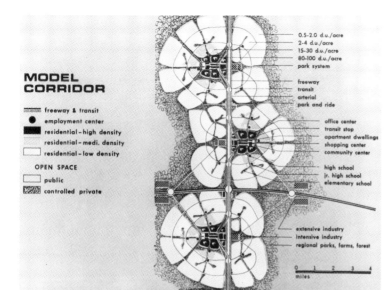

MODEL CORRIDOR

- freeway & transit
- ● employment center
- ■ residential – high density
- residential – medi. density
- □ residential – low density

OPEN SPACE
- □ public
- controlled private

0.5-2.0 d.u./acre
2-4 d.u./acre
15-30 d.u./acre
80-100 d.u./acre
park system

freeway
transit
arterial
park and ride

office center
transit stop
apartment dwellings
shopping center
community center

high school
jr. high school
elementary school

extensive industry
intensive industry
regional parks, farms, forest

0 1 2 3 4
miles

119 Washington, D.C.,
model corridor, "Year 2000
Plan," published 1961.

120 Reston, Virginia, Lake Anne Village Center, 1970.

121 Columbia, Maryland, city
center area, 1972.

122 Columbia, Maryland, 1973,
the air-conditioned mall.

123 Columbia, Maryland, Wild
Lake Village area, 1972.

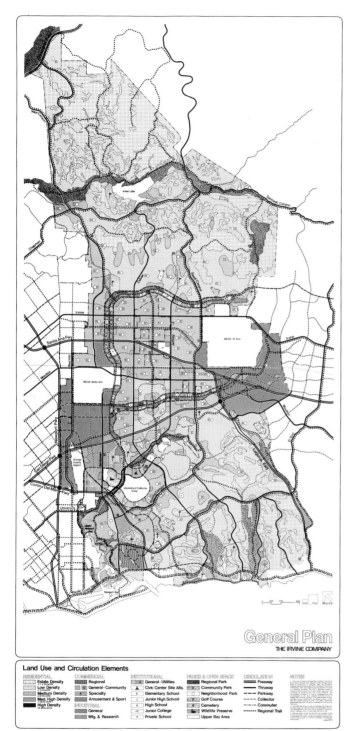

124 Irvine, California, 1973,
general plan.

125 Irvine, California, 1973,
view of Newport Center.

Land Use and Circulation Elements

RESIDENTIAL
- Estate Density
- Low Density
- Medium Density
- Med. High Density
- High Density

COMMERCIAL
- Regional
- General - Community
- Specialty
- Amusement & Sport

INDUSTRIAL
- General
- Mfg. & Research

INSTITUTIONAL
- General - Utilities
- Civic Center Site Alts.
- Elementary School
- Junior High School
- High School
- Junior College
- Private School

PARKS & OPEN SPACE
- Regional Park
- Community Park
- Neighborhood Park
- Golf Course
- Cemetery
- Wildlife Preserve
- Upper Bay Area

CIRCULATION
- Freeway
- Thruway
- Parkway
- Collector
- Commuter
- Regional Trail

NOTES

126 Audubon, New York, land
use map, 1972.

127 1970 model of S.U.N.Y.
campus at Buffalo-Amherst.
Hideo Sasaki, architect for
State University
Construction Fund
(copyright).

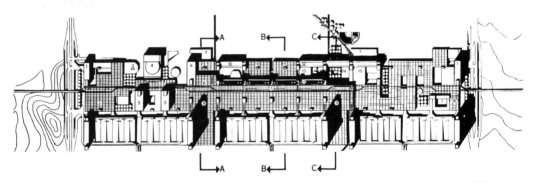

Roof Plan

Systems Plan

128 Billerica, New Town Proposal of Harvard University Group, 1969.

NOTES

Works referred to in abbreviated form may be found in the bibliography.

Preface **1** Statement made by Giedion in the course of his lectures at the Zurich ETH (Swiss Federal Institute of Technology) in 1953, which I attended as a student. Similar statements appear in his *Space/Time, and Architecture,* see 4th edition, 1962, pp. vii and 6.

2 In this volume areas are given in hectares (ha.) rather than acres in order to facilitate comparison. 1 ha. = 2.47 acres

Chapter 1 **1** The notion of "the City as an act of will" was coined by Bacon who uses it to define the evolution of urban form as the succession of interrelated decisions. In this sense a planned new town with a preconceived form or master plan is creation as an "act of will" par excellence.

2 See Fourastié.

Chapter 2 **1** As quoted by Dr. Ernesto Silva, president of the *Instituto Historico e Geografico do Distrito Federal* (Brasilia), in his talk at Columbia University in 1969; sponsored by the Institute of Latin American Studies, Kempton Webb, and myself.

2 Kite.

3 Lampl, p. 31.

4 *Ibid.,* p. 19.

5 Diodorus Siculus, writing around 30 B.C., claims to have learned from the official in charge of the census rolls of his time—i.e., three hundred years after the foundation of Alexandria—that the city's population numbered 300,000 free persons; adding women and slaves this would yield a million inhabitants. However, computing on size and potential density of the town, 300,000 for the total population seems a more reasonable figure. See also, Ward-Perkins, pp. 19–21.

6 Egli, Ernst, *Geschichte des Städtebaues,* II, p. 283.

7 Creswell, pp. 163. For dimensions I follow Creswell and Herzfeld. Le Strange gives somewhat different dimensions: the diameter as 2,800 m. and an area of 65 ha. See Le Strange, *Baghdad in the time of the Abbasid Khalifate* (Oxford University Press, 1924).

8 Quoting Le Strange, Egli gives some of the original sources. See Egil, *Geschichte,* II, p. 284.

9 The idea of radioconcentric formal planning may have been derived from the Assyrians. Creswell points out that on one of Layard's tablets, found in Nineveh, a perfectly circular military camp is shown. However, the older Hittite town of Sam'al (Zinçirli) built in the ninth century B.C. already shows a nearly perfect circular wall with three gates, a diameter of 700 m. and an area of 36.8 ha (See Lampl, p. 46).

10 Excavations have proved that the Chou-Wang-Cheng capital was in fact built on an even larger scale. Its north wall was 2,890 m. in length. (See Hiraoka and Imai, p. 14).

11 The Imperial city of Lo-Yang was a rectangle of 6 li × 9 li. Remnants of the walls measure 2.6 km. × 3.8 km.; area 888 ha. (See Tange, K., Kawazoe, N., *Ise: Prototype of Japanese Architecture,* M.I.T. Press, 1965. 200).

12 Width of the E–W avenue separating the Imperial City from the Palace: 500 m. or 1,650 ft. (more than the Champs Elysées in Paris); major N–S avenues 150 m. or 450 ft.; minor E–W avenues 70 m. or 250 ft.

13 Chung, H.C., "Capital Cities of China," pp. 1–64.

14 An important event was the doubling of the area of Ferrara in 1492 according to plans by Biagio Rossetti, whom Zevi considers the first city planner in the modern sense. However, Argan rightly observes that the expansion was prompted by demographic and economic considerations rather than the need to adapt the town to governmental or court functions (Argan, p. 31).

15 Argan erroneously states that the main streets run into three corners of the square. The main streets run into the center of three sides and the corners are, in fact, closed (Argan, p. 111).

16 It exerted great influence, however, on the plans of the eighteenth-century district capitals of *Bogorodsk, Tula, Rostow-Jaroslavl,* etc. and can even be detected in the formalistic planning of the Stalinist period (1930–50).

17 18,038 in 1790. Thomas Pemberton, *Topographical and Historical Description of Boston,* 1794.

18 One weakness of L'Enfant's plan remains that Maryland Avenue could never become the functional equivalent of Pennsylvania Avenue; another was his neglect of the Potomac riverfront as a potential area for center-city animation.

19 Inspired by the famous "finger plan" of Copenhagen (1947). The spines would be rapid transit lines and expressways separated by green "wedges."

20 With 180,000 inhabitants, Canberra is now the largest inland city in Australia. Due to a growth rate of about 9 percent, the town should reach the half million mark before the end of the century.

21 In 1965–70 the planning commission examined options to seek out a plan concept that would serve a population up to one million. A Y-shaped town structure was chosen, providing for growth along three rapid-transit corridors. These corridors will integrate the new satellite towns of Woden, Belconnen, Tuggeranong, and Gunghalin—each designed to accommodate a population of 100,000 to 170,000 people (see Pl. 16).

22 On alternate projects for Brasilia see Evenson, *Two Brazilian Capitals* and Caixeita, Donaldo, "Como Brasilia Poderia ter sido," in *Correo Brasilense,* May 28, 1971.

Chapter 3

1 Mohenjo Daro was built around 1700 B.C. The town area of 138 ha. is a fairly regular rectangle of 1,100 × 1,250 m. divided into twelve sectors by straight avenues equipped with covered sewers.

2 The character *village* was derived from a hieroglyphic symbol of man kneeling under a square enclosure, implying rectangular walls. The character *capital* derives from the image of a gate tower. The character *state* consists of signs meaning, "protection of the people by military force" enclosed in a square. See Chung, p. 2 and Trewartha, p. 69.

3 The Incas founded numerous new towns in regions where there were no suitable centers for their administration. Hardoy mentions Incahusai, Viracochampa, Ollantaytambo. Most impressive is the very regular layout of Viracochampa with an area of 40 ha. See Hardoy, *Urban Planning in Pre-Columbian America.*

4 The area of the island city of Tenochtitlan was extended by land reclamation with the help of floats cut of the local *chinampa* reed. Five such floats anchored side by side yielded a regular town lot of 35 m. × 35 m. confined within a checkerboard grid of streets and canals. An Aztec plan prepared shortly after the conquest shows this pattern clearly, and it has also been described by numerous *conquistadores.*

5 Henry Frankfort, "Town Planning in Ancient Mesopotamia," in *Town Planning Review,* July 1950.

6 Zernaki Tepe was laid out with a checkerboard plat of 5 m. (except for two 7 m. wide streets) defining 35 m. square blocks each divided into four equal lots. See Lampl, p. 113.

7 In Chapter II, 8 and VII, 11 of his *Politics,* Aristotle specifically refers to Hippodamus as the planner of Piraeus (475 B.C.). However, examples of pre-Hippodamean grids are numerous. See Ward-Perkins, pp. 22–23.

8 Plutarch credits Alexander himself with seventy. See Ward-Perkins, p. 20.

9 Wycherley R. E., *How the Greeks Built Cities,* New York, Doubleday, 1969. See also Ward-Perkins, pp. 14–18.

10 *Stratagematon libri IV.* This point is also made by Boethius.

11 Good aerial photographs of "centuriato" have been published by Bradford, John, *Ancient Landscapes: Studies in Field Archeology,* London, 1957.

12 See Reischauer, E. O. and Fairbank, J. K., *East Asia, the Great Tradition,* Boston, Houghton Mifflin, 1960, pp. 51, 81; and Gutkind, E. A., *Evolution of Environment,* Boston, Houghton Mifflin, 1960, p. 246.

13 This town system corresponds to the Roman hierarchy of *castra, oppida, colonia,* etc. and survives in modern Japan as the *machi-shi-to* classification of towns by their size.

14 The size of the *Fangs* varied since the noble *Shih* were assigned lots eight times larger than the other classes. (Shih lots were about 1/4th acre, the regular size lot 1/32nd acre or 25 × 50 ft.) The size of the Fangs of Changan varied from 530 m. × 492 to 983 × 833 m. The most common size was 681 × 492 m.—about 33 ha.

15 This extreme rationality in land allocation later led in Japan to the development of standard house plans based on the model of the *tatami* floor mats of about 1 m. × 2 m. size. The floor area of two tatami was considered the minimum adequate living space for a person. About 250 tatami sizes correspond to the minimum town lot of 15 m. × 30 m. thirty-two lots form a town block or Cho; 4 Chos a ward or Ho (128 households) and 4 Ho a neighborhood or Bo.

16 P. Hofer in Hofer and Galantay, *The Zähringer New Towns,* Zurich, Swiss Fed. Inst. of Technology Publications, 1966. Saalman (p. 114) is mistaken in stating, with reference to the Roman colonial settlements, that "enough of them survived to serve as models."

17 See Pirenne.

18 Andrew II of Hungary called in the Teutonic Order in 1211 to establish fifteen new towns in Transylvania, both for frontier defense and to develop the mining trade, while Duke Przemislaw of Poland called in Germans to build such trading centers as Poznan in 1253.

19 St. Thomas Aquinas, *De Regime Principorum,* 7.1., *Summa Theologia* Q.91 Art. 2.

20 The meticulous study by Beresford, enumerates 74 new towns for Wales alone and puts the number of English new towns founded before 1300 at 152; 113 in Gascony. Beresford states that Edward I called a regular meeting of the Parliament in 1297 to advise him "how to devise, order and array new towns to the greatest profit of Ourselves and the merchants." See also Egli *Geschichte* . . . and Hofer.

21 Saalman, p. 114.

22 In Gascony some towns founded by Edward I still had no walls in the time of Edward III. In fact, two thirds of the "bastides" of southern France were *never* provided with defenses. See: Trabut-Cussac, J. P., "Bastides ou Forteresses?" in *Le Moyen Age,* LX, 1954, pp. 81–135.

23 Thirty-seven percent of all English plantations; seventy-one percent of all foundations in Gascony, and fifteen percent of all plans of towns founded by the counts of Toulouse, according to Beresford.

24 Of fifty-five Apulian towns ten belong to this category. See: Minchilli, Enzo: *Classificazione delle Citta in Puglia,* Inst. Poligrafico dello Stato, Rome, 1958.

25 For a discussion of this see my article on "Medieval New Towns," in *Progressive Architecture,* August, 1968, pp. 126–137.

26 Around 1493 Francisco di Giorgio Martini systematically examined all possible block and street systems: orthogonal, concentric and even curvilinear. Lorimi and Scamozzi also paid some attention to the internal organization of a town into parishes each equipped with a market square like the Venetian "campi." See also De la Croix, pp. 39–55.

27 After some experimentation with radiating street-patterns, with their inefficient blocks and wasteful street layout—the seventeenth century once again returned to sensible orthogonality, as in Vauban's *Neuf Brisach,* 1694. A unique example of an efficient hexagonal town plan is Grammichele, founded in 1693 by Prince Carlo Maria Caraffa. A hexagonal "Piazza Principale" is surrounded by seven concentric ringroads. Attached to the sides of the hexagon are six rectangular *borghi,* each with its own administrator or *curatore.*

28 H. De la Croix, "Palmanova: A Study in Sixteenth Century Urbanism," *Saggi e memorie di storia dell'arte,* V, Florence, 1967; *Military Considerations,* pp. 49–52.

29 The "Irish Society" was a colonizing company created by the Council of the City of London. In 1609 a regional development plan was prepared for the six counties of the province of Ulster; twenty-three new town sites were designated. Derry and Coleraine were planned in 1611.

30 For example during the governorship of Per Brahe in Finland (1637–1654), the number of Finnish towns doubled from 14 to 28. Lilius, Henrik, *Der Pekkatori in Raahe,* Univ. of Helsinki, 1967, pp. 16–18. For Danish foundations see Rasmussen. The Swedish "New Town Policy" in the Baltic is brilliantly presented by Gerhard Eimer.

31 A publication on this interesting group of planned settlements is being prepared by Henry A. Millon.

32 Hardoy points out that nine of the ten most populous towns of Latin America were founded prior to 1580. The exception is Montevideo.

33 In general a *caballería* was five times larger than a *peonería.* In Columbia their respective sizes were: caballería 816 × 406 m. or 33 ha., *Peonería* 6.6 ha. See Martinez.

34 The layout of the colonial towns began with the *plaza mayor.* The focus of the plan was thus not a building but empty space destined to remain empty. As Robert Ricard observes: "The Hispano-American town is a Plaza surrounded by streets and buildings, rather than a pattern of buildings and streets with a square in its middle." According to the Laws the *plaza mayor* was to be rectangular in shape and no less than 200 × 300 ft. nor larger than 800 × 532 ft. However, in this respect very few town plans followed the instructions: most *plazas mayores* are square rather than elongated. One exception is Puebla in Mexico with its plaza dating from 1541, of a size of 240 × 175 *varas* or about 117 m. × 200 m. or 2.34 ha.

35 Such palaces are now often occupied by political parties or clubs, in general local pressure groups.

36 This can be observed on the plan of Mendoza (Plate 44a). Franciscans in the SW corner, Dominicans in the NW, Mercedarians in the NE, and a hospital in the SE corner.

37 Such *barrios* often harbored separate ethnic groups or Spanish settlers of different provenience, i.e. in Merida (Yucatan) founded in 1542 one *barrio* was reserved for Spaniards, and one each assigned to the local Mayas, another to the Aztec alllies of the Spaniards and the fourth to negroes and mulattoes.

38 J. Reps in *The Making of Urban America.*

39 Stanislawski, Dan, "The Origin and Spread of the Grid Pattern Town," *The Geographic Review,* XLVI, 1946, pp. 105–120. An important work on castrametation is the "Siete Partidas" of King Alfonso X. It is interesting to note also that 150 codices of Vegetius' "Rei Militaris Instituta" survive to this day while only twelve codex copies of Vitruvius exist dating between the ninth and twelfth centuries and only eleven more from the period between the thirteenth and the invention of printing, according to Choisy, *Vitruve,* Paris, 1908. The first printed copy of Vitruvius found its way to Mexico in 1550 (Manuel Toussaint, *Arquitectura Religiosa,* Mexico, Imprenta Universitaria, 1956).

40 Stanislawski, "The Origin and Spread of the Grid-Pattern," *Geographical Review,* 1947.

41 Kubler, George, *Mexican Architecture in the XVI Century,* New Haven: Yale University Press, 1948.

42 One of the first towns of the reconquest was Avila, completely rebuilt after its destruction in 1085, after a plan by Florence de Pitengue and settled with 3,000 Frenchmen from Burgundy. Numerous new towns were founded in twelfth-century Navarre and in thirteenth-century Aragon—the best known is Villareal (1233). See Torres-Balbas et al.

43 Francesch Eiximenis, *El Crestià,* Libre Dotzen, was printed in 1484, his *Regiment de la Cosa Publica* in 1499—just in time to be of use in the colonization of the Americas. For a detailed discussion of Eiximenis' work and his influence on Latin-American planning see my paper on "The Traditional Structure of Latin American Towns," in the Series of the Institut für die Theorie und Geschichte der Architektur, ETH, Zurich 1974.

44 Eiximenis' town was to have a side length of 807 m. and an area of 65 ha. It provided for 1,600 dwelling units, and if one adds the number of monks, nuns, and clerics in the various religious establishments plus the garrison and personnel of the palace one arrives at a figure of 10,000 for the population. As to land use his ideal town assigned 25 percent of its area to streets and plazas, 63 percent to residential use, and the remaining 12 percent to public buildings and institutions.

45 Reps points out that such was the authority of this corpus of Laws that even after the disintegration of the Spanish colonial empire the successor states continued to apply it in laying out new towns. See also Torres-Balbas et al.

46 Both the foundation procedure and the resulting physical layout of some *barriadas* resembles the instructions and adhere to the spirit of the instructions of the Laws.

47 See Bridenbaugh.

48 Reps, pp. 95–103.

49 Reps (p. 163) relates this disposition to Newcourt's plan for the rebuilding of London (1666). It is more likely that Penn was influenced by the functionalist trend at Leyden under Simon Stevin, whom Penn undoubtedly met on one of his trips to Holland. Compare the plan of Philadelphia with Stevin's ideal plan (Plate 40).

50 Bacon (p. 202) reproduces an ideal plan by Cataneo (1567) in which he sees a possible model for Savannah. Newcourt's plan for London (1666) also has similarities in its repetition of identically organized wards.

51 Blokhine, P. N., in "Provision of Welfare and Cultural Facilities and Public Utilities in the Cities of the USSR," *Paper no. 31* submitted at the U.N. Conference on Metropolitan Development, Stockholm, Sept. 1961.

52 See Malisz.

Chapter 4 **1** This approach is not based on balanced development but on the more dynamic strategy of "disjointed incrementalism." For a discussion of alternate development strategies see Albert O. Hirschman, *The Strategy of Economic Development* (New Haven: Yale University Press, 1958), and Albert O. Hirschman and Charles E. Lindblom, "Economic Development, Research and Development, Policy Making: Some Converging Views," in *Behavioural Science,* vol. 7, April 1962.

2 Turkish workers of the petrochemical plant at Aliaga commute 80 km. from Izmir; Venezuelan steelworkers in Ciudad Guayana used to commute from as far as Ciudad Bolivar, 100 km. away. Such long-distance commuting can be extremely costly to management: Venezuelan labor law compels industry to reimburse the workers for the transportation and provides half-time pay for journeys longer than 2 kms.

3 In post-World War II Western Europe few new industrial towns have been founded: in Britain one might mention Dawley and Cumbran, located in mining zones; and Newton, Aycliffe, Washington, Peterlee, and Telford, which seem to have the primary purpose of revitalizing lagging old industrial regions.
 In Germany, Marl was created in 1946 to provide another focus for the new northern growth area of the Ruhr-coal conurbation. The town is known for its innovative architecture and is approaching a population of 100,000. Another new town in the Ruhr is Wulfen—planned in 1965 for a population of 50,000. In France the town of Mourenx, with 12,000 inhabitants, serves the exploitation of the gas of Lacq in the lower Pyrenees, and the creation of a larger new town may result from the vast new metallurgical complex in the Bay of Fos near Marseille.

4 This town is being developed by the Aluminum Company of Canada. Planners were Albert Mayer and Clarence Stein, who proposed a garden city layout in the harsh climate. All material except timber had to be imported. The proposed population of the town was 30 to 50,000; the 1959 population was 12,250.

5 This method was developed in 1939 by Homer Hoyt. For a critical discussion of the "Basic-Nonbasic" concept see: Hans Blumenfled "The Economic Base of the Metropolis," in *Journal of the American Institute of Planners,* Vol. 21, no. 4, 1955.
 In the Soviet Union the future population is calculated on the basis of the following rule-of-thumb formula:

$$P = \frac{100 \times A}{100 - (B + C)}$$

in which A is the absolute number of those working in the basic or town-forming industries
B is the proportion of the population employed in public service institutions
C is the proportion of the nonemployed in percentage of the total population.

Source: GIPROGOR (State Town Planning Institute of the State Committee on Building Affairs of the Council of Ministers of the RSFSR—Russian Soviet Federated Socialist Republic), Contract No. 1595, Moscow, 1969.

6 Lampl, pp. 30–31.

7 A factual study of this early workers' housing project is E. Trinconato's article, "La Marinarezza di Venezia," ("Early Public Housing in Venice") in *Urbanistica* Nos. 42. 43.

8 See Choay.

9 Coolidge, John, *Mill and Mansion,* New York, Russell, 1942.

10 Creese, p. 46.

11 See Wiebenson.

12 Garnier's concept was socialistic: not only did he propose that society should have full ownership of land, but he also advocated free water supply, free distribution of bread and milk, and free medical services. See Wiebenson.

13 See Evenson.

14 *Revolutsiia i Kultura,* No. 1, January 15, 1930, as quoted in Parkins; for the early planning of Stalingrad see Khevsin, T., "Kak My Stroim Sotsialisticheskii Stalingrad," in the same issue of *Revolutsiia.* For the replanning of Stalingrad, see Poliakov, N.K., "Planirovka Stalingrada," in *Arkhitektura S.S.S.R.,* No. 6, Moscow, 1944.

15 See Note 51, Chapter 3.

16 For a good discussion of Polish and Hungarian new towns see P. Merlin, *Nouvelles Planification et Urbanisme en Pologne,* Chapters V and VI.

17 On the origins of the planning of Salzgitter and Wolfsburg see Teut and Meibeyer.

18 This organization closely resembles the one proposed by Kung Fu Tse (See p. 26). See also Teut, Alfred Speer, *Inside the Third Reich,* New York, Macmillan, 1970 and Adolf Hitler, *Secret Conversations, 1941–1944,* New York, Octagon, n.d.

19 Wolfsburg: In 1938 the legal basis for the new community was created by the amalgamation of nine previously separate administrative entities and by exempting the city from all local zoning and building codes.

20 Migrant workers started to arrive in substantial numbers in 1962. Their housing presents a problem: at present about half of them are concentrated in a plant-owned camp north of the canal and adjacent to the Volkswagen works.

21 The people of Wolfsburg take great pride in the modern layout and equipment of the town. Civic pride is also boosted by the prestigious art award presented each year by the City. Wolfsburgers are considered "arrogant" by outsiders.

22 Site selection was approved in January, 1967. The draft Master Plan was submitted in April, 1968. The site is on an elevation of 1,620–1,880 m. Summer temperatures reach 42 centigrade; winter can be as low as −16 centigrade.

23 The Aria-Mehr steel works employs, initially, 7,000 workers to produce yearly 600,000 tons of steel. Their number will rise with increased output to 10,000 and eventually to 14,000, according to GIPROMES (Soviet State Planning Agency for Heavy Industry).

24 The ratio of employment to total population is 18 percent in Abadan and 27 percent in Teheran.

25 The CVG or Corporación Venezolana de Guayana was created in 1960 by President Betancourt. It is directed by General Rafael Alfonzo Ravard. Building the new town is only one of the many tasks of the Corporation, which is also responsible for the management of the steel plant, for regional development, including the electrification of the Caroní River and a vast agricultural scheme in the Orinoco delta.

26 The CVG engaged the assistance of the Joint Center of Urban Studies of the Massachusetts Institute of Technology, and Harvard Professor Lloyd Rodwin headed the advisory team. Wilhelm Viggo von Moltke directed the urban-design group.

27 This figure was based on the provision of 100,000 jobs. One-third in basic industry, two-thirds in secondary industries and services. It soon became clear that lack of skilled labor slowed down industrial expansion.

28 For a straightforward discussion of the confusion created in physical planning due to the frequent revisions of the economic targets, see the article of A. Penfold, "Planning Urban Growth. . . ." (chapter 9), in Rodwin.

29 For the emerging dichotomy between the two sides of the city and the conflict situations between the CVG (Corporación Venezolana de Guayana) and the "autochthonous groups," see Lisa R. Peattie, in *The View from the Barrio,* Ann Arbor, The University of Michigan Press, 1968. For use of the computer model in Ciudad Guayana, see Penfold, Anthony, "Ciudad Guayana—Planning a New City," in the *Town Planning Review,* January, 1967, pp. 226–235.

30 As a civic center, Alta Vista suffered from the refusal of the leaders of the municipal government to leave their power base in San Felix in order to move to the new center. Robert Wood pointed out that such a move would be interpreted as a power shift to the new residents on the west side. They would not have objected to moving to the bridgehead location on Punta Vista. See Wood, Corporación Venezolana de Guayana (CVG), August 14, 1963.

31 The advocates of the "single-city strategy" correctly predicted the dire consequences of locating the town center on Alta Vista. See E. Galantay, J. Perez-Canto, and H. Weber, "Evaluation of Sites for Focal Structures," CVG Staff Paper No. E-79, August, 1963. On goal conflicts between planners and the local population see also my article, "Planificacion a largo plazo vs. necesidades inmediates" in *Resumenes 28a Reunión, Sociedad para la Antropología Aplicada,* Eds. S. Camara and L. Comitas, Museo Nacional de Antropología, Ciudad de Mexico, 1969.

32 This conclusion is reinforced by the experience in Beer Sheba, Israel, where the proposed new center is unable to compete with the vitality of the old town center of Turkish origin. See E. Spiegel, *New Towns in Israel,* New York, Praeger, 1967, pp. 140–143.

33 The residents of Ciudad Guayana will have to spend 17 percent of their available income for transportation. This is the same percentage as in Los Angeles, but taken out of the much lower income of the workers of Ciudad Guayana it hurts more.

In other U.S. cities transportation cost is less: Chicago 12 percent; New York 8 percent of available income.

Chapter 5 **1** The first modern formulation of a decongestion strategy is contained in a memorandum by Leonardo da Vinci addressed to Ludovico Sforza (Bibl. Institut de France Ms. B. Fol. 16). Following the 1485 pestilence, which claimed 50,000 lives in Milan, Leonardo proposed the decongestion of the already large city by the creation of satellite towns of no more than 10,000 inhabitants each. An original feature of this proposal was the recommendation of a multilevel layout of the town center with the top level reserved for pedestrians with direct access to the shops, and the lower level assigned to wheeled traffic—both for the movement of goods and for trash removal —with stairs connecting the two levels at convenient distances.

Some two-level streets exist in planned medieval towns such as Bern, Thun, and Chester, with pedestrian arcades elevated above the carriage road from which the goods delivery to the shops is handled. However, the idea of a consequent separation of vehicular traffic from pedestrians does not reoccur until the second generation British new towns, with the proposal for Hook, and the focal structure of Cumbernauld (See pp. 59–60).

2 To restrict the growth of Moscow an "internal passport system" was introduced in the USSR in 1935. Nevertheless, the Moscow area rapidly outgrew the maximum size envisaged by the 1935 general plan. See P. Hall, *The World Cities,* pp. 158–181.

3 On "growth pole strategy" see L. Rodwin in *Nations and Cities* (Boston: Houghton Mifflin, 1970), and John Friedman in "The Changing Pattern of Urbanization in Venezuela," in Rodwin, *Planning Urban Growth,* Chapter 2, pp. 40–59.

4 On the "second Paris," le "Paris bis," see P. Merlin, *Les Villes Nouvelles,* p. 311.

5 On Mexico's Ciudad Paralela see *La Marcha a la Provincia,* by Ing. Victor Vila and Professor F. Escalante-Escalante (Ciudad de Mexico: Calitlan S.A., 1967). Report prepared in 1968.

6 On El Tuy see Llewelyn-Davis, Weeks, et al., "The Tuy Medio," The M.O.P. Direccion de Planeamiento, República de Venezuela.

7 On Le Vésinet see F. Choay, fig. 43 and p. 28. The developed area consisted of 436 ha.

8 The best authority on the *Ciudad Lineal* is George Collins. See his articles in the *Journal of the Society of Architectural Historians,* XVIII, "The Ciudad Lineal of Madrid," May, 1959, pp. 74–93 and "Lineal Planning Throughout the World," Oct., 1959, pp. 38–53, and in the whole issue of *Forum* (Amsterdam) XX, No. 5, 1968. Also, Choay, p. 99.

9 Official definition by the Garden Cities and Town Planning Association, adopted in 1919. See Osborn and Whittick, p. 11.

10 Letchworth, see Choay, p. 108 and figs. 79–81.

11 For a recent adaptation of the Gloeden model, see Plate 23, the Roberto plan for Brasilia.

12 For a critique of the neighborhood concept, see Isaacs and Tyrwhitt.

13 Abercrombie first proposed a greenbelt in his 1943 report to the London County Council. But note also the prior proposal of a greenbelt for Moscow (1935, General Plan). A greenbelt was planned around Vienna in the early twentieth century; see G. R. and C. C. Collins, *Camillo Sitte and the Birth of Modern City Planning* (New York: Random House, 1964), pp. 42, 96, 130, 143, 211.

14 Telford and Redditch were created to relieve Birmingham; Skelemersdale and Runcorn to draw population from Liverpool and Merseyside; Warrington from Manchester; Washington from Newcastle. The Scottish new towns of Cumbernauld, East Kilbridge, Glenrothes, Irvine, and Livingstone are all aimed to decongest Glasgow. See also, *The New Towns of Britain* (London: British Information Services, HMSM, 1973).

15 The first postwar pedestrian precinct was the "Lijnbaan" in Rotterdam, designed in 1955.

16 The idea of high density "sinews" had its origins in the 1930s in linear city theory. Since then the concept has been put to test in Toulouse-Le Mirail (See Candilis-Josic-Woods, p. 187) and has been proposed for Reston, Va., the first project of Milton Keynes, Evry, etc. The concept of "activity spines," i.e., the concentration of public buildings and amenities along preferential movement axes is related to the idea of "sinews," but it does not necessarily imply concentrated residential densities. Examples: Tuggenarong (Canberra), Irvine, Calif., and Evry.

17 For a French view on Cumbernauld, see: Guertin.

18 Melvin M. Webber, "Order in Diversity: Community without Propinquity," in Lowdon Wingo, Jr., ed., *Cities and Space: The Future Use of Urban Land,* Baltimore, Johns Hopkins, 1963. Also, "The Urban Place and the Nonplace Urban Realm," in Webber, M. M., *Explorations into Urban Structure,* Philadelphia, U. of Pa. Press, 1971, pp. 79–153.

19 For an attack on low-density new towns see the entire issue of the *Architectural Review,* October, 1973. One article points out that of a total of 54 million acres of land in Britain, 33.5 million acres are subject to various constraints to development. When completed, Milton Keynes will have an overall population density of 11.3 persons per acre. Spread out evenly at this density 55 million Britons would require 5.5 million acres of developed land, or one out of every five acres not restricted to some other use (mines, scenic areas, etc.). Although America still has enough space to waste, if all Britons were to be housed at the low density of Milton Keynes, urban sprawl would take up one of every five available acres.

20 The city of Stockholm owns most of the land within its boundaries. The city area is in itself quite big—18,600 ha. of land and 2,700 ha. of water. In addition to this, the city owned in 1971 50,000 ha. more land outside its boundaries. Compare this to the size of the city of Paris of 10,500 ha. only, with 3 million inhabitants.

21 The 1975 population of Greater Tokyo was estimated as 28 million, of whom 16 million will live in the outer ring area. To accomodate this growth, fifteen sites for satellite towns were designated in 1963 for populations of 150,000 to 670,000. The creation of 30 additional satellite towns was proposed. The 1958 "Law for Town Development in the National Capital

Region," provides the legal mechanism for the development of satellite towns. Under this law the central government will provide funds and technical assistance to local authorities for new town building, and the government can also advance funds to recognized private developers. A 1959 law restricts the establishment of further industries or educational institutions within the built-up central Tokyo area.

22 To be built at a distance of 144 km. from Tokyo near Mt. Fuji, on 40,000 ha. of government-owned land. The project envisages the transfer of some eighty government agencies employing 180,000 civil servants. See City Planning Association of Japan, *Giant Tokyo:* Tokyo, 1963, and Tokyo Metropolitan Government: *An Outline of Ten-Year Plan for Government of Tokyo,* Tokyo, 1963, *An Administrative Perspective of Tokyo: City Planning,* Tokyo, 1972.

23 The Russians use this term to denote planned satellite towns, as well as towns in the outer ring of the metropolis which developed independently but gradually acquired a satellite function.

24 For a discussion of the growth of Moscow, see Peter Hall, *The World Cities,* pp. 158–181.

25 A. A. Afitchenko: "About the reaction and development of satellite towns around large cities," in "News from Scientific Departments," *Stroitelśtvo i Arkhitektura,* Moscow, 1962, No. 2.

26 N. V. Baranov, "Building of New Towns," position paper no. 11 presented at the U.N. Symposium on the Planning and Development of New Towns. Moscow, 24 August to 7 September, 1964. See also paper presented by G. Muranova at the W.H.O. Conference on Health Aspects of Urbanization, December, 1973, Stuttgart.

27 In 1954, 22 percent of Paris dwelling units lacked running water, and a 1961 survey showed that 31 percent of the units in the Paris region lacked a private water toilet or washstand. Only one unit in five had a bathtub or shower. "Une Enquête par Sondage sur le Logement," *Etudes Statistiques,* no. 2, Paris, 1957, and *Annuaires Statistiques Abrégés de la Région Parisienne,* Paris, 1961.

28 On Toulouse-Le Mirail, see Candilis-Josic-Woods.

29 This handy term was coined by Paul and Percival Goodman in *Communitas,* pp. 125, ff.

30 This term was invented by James Rouse, the developer of Columbia, Maryland, to characterize the unstructured suburb in contrast to a planned community.

31 On planning and the growth of Reston and Columbia, see my articles in *The Nation,* December, 1966, pp. 652 and 714.

32 See the article by Richard Brooks, "Social Planning in Columbia," *Journal of the American Institute of Planners,* November 1971, p. 373; Robert B. Zehner, "Neighborhoods and Community Satisfaction in New Towns," op. cit., p. 379.

33 On Irvine, California, see William R. Mason, *The Irvine Company on the Road to a Model Urban Environment,* Irvine, September, 1973.

34 In 1968 median family income in the United States was

$8,000. A 1969 survey found median incomes in Reston of $20,000 and in Columbia, Maryland of $17,000.

35 The lowest figure proposed is an increase by 55 million Americans in 30 years. Anthony Downs, "Alternative Forms of Future Urban Growth in the United States," *Journal of the American Institute of Planners,* January, 1970, p. 3.

36 Rodwin, Lloyd and Susskind, Lawrence, "New Communities and Urban Growth Strategies," presented at the American Institute of Architects' Conference on New Communities, Washington, D.C.

37 On Columbia, Maryland, see Hoppenfeld; on Reston, see "Reston Quarterly Facts Sheets."

38 On Audubon-Amherst and the complicated negotiations between public developer and local communities in Audubon-Amherst, see the Contract Summary published by the New York Urban Development Corporation.

39 On "Black New Towns," see my article in *Progressive Architecture,* August 1968, pp. 126–137, and note 32 above.

BIBLIOGRAPHY

General

Abercrombie, Patrick, "The Rise and Decline of Neighborhood Planning," *Housing Review,* V. 1956, 143–145.

Blumenfeld, Hans, *The Modern Metropolis,* Cambridge, MIT Press, 1966.

Chapin, F. Stuart, Jr., "How Big Should a City Be?", *Planning Outlook,* II, 1950, 37–48.

Chermayeff, Serge, and Tzonis, Alexander, *Shape of Community,* Baltimore, Pelican Penguin Books, 1971.

Doxiades, Constantinos, *Ekistics,* London, Hutchinson & Co., 1968.

Duncan, Otis Dudley, "Optimum Size of Cities," in Hatt, Paul K., and Reiss, Albert J. (eds.), *Cities and Society,* Glencoe, Illinois, Free Press, 1967.

Egli, Ernest, *Die Neue Stadt,* Erlenbach-Zurich, Verlag fur Architektur, 1951.

Ekistics, XVIII, No. 108, November, 1964.

Fritsch, Theodor, *Die Stadt der Zukunft,* Leipzig, Hammer, 1896, 2nd ed., 1912.

Goodman, Paul and Percival, *Communitas,* 2nd revised edition, New York, Random House, 1960. Originally published by University of Chicago Press, 1947.

Humbert, Ricardo C., *La Ciudad Hexagonal,* Buenos Aires, Vasca Ekin, 1944.

Lang, S., "The Ideal City from Plato to Howard, *Architectural Review,* CXII, August 1952, 90–101.

Lavedan, Pierre, *Histoire d'Urbanisme,* Paris, Henri Laurens, 1926–1952, 3 volumes (especially vol. III).

Le Corbusier, *La Ville Radieuse,* Paris, 1933. (English: *The Radiant City,* New York, The Orion Press, 1964.)

Lichtfield, N., "Cost Benefits Analysis in Urban Expansion. A Case Study: Peterborough," in *Regional Studies,* September, 1969, 123–155.

Lillibridge, Robert M. "Urban size: an Assessment," *Land Economics,* XXVIII, November, 1952, 341–352.

Lynch, Kevin, "The Form of Cities," *Scientific American,* CXC, April, 1954, 20. 54–63.

Lynch, Kevin and Rodwin, Lloyd, "A Theory of Urban Form," *J. Amer. Inst. of Planners,* XXIV, No. 4, 1958, 201–214.

Malisz, B., *La Formation des systèmes d'habitat,* Dunod, Paris, 1972.

Merlin, Pierre, *Les Villes nouvelles,* 2nd edition, 1972, Paris, Presses Universitaires de France.

Mumford, Lewis, "The Neighborhood and the Neighborhood Unit," *The Planning Review,* XXIV, 1954, 256–270.

Mumford, Lewis, *The Story of Utopias,* Compass Books, New York, Viking Press, 1962. Originally published New York, Boni and Liveright, 1922.

Planning of Metropolitan Areas and New Towns, New York, United Nations, 1967.

Rasmussen, Steen Eiler, "Neighborhood Planning," *The Planning Review,* XXVII, 1957, 197–218.

Reiner, Thomas A., *The Place of the Ideal Community in Urban Planning,* University of Pennsylvania Press, 1963.

Rodwin, Lloyd (ed.), et al. *The Future Metropolis,* New York, George Braziller, 1961.

Rodwin, Lloyd, *Nations and Cities,* Boston, Houghton Mifflin, 1970, (especially Chapter VII).

Rosenau, Helen, *The Ideal City,* London, Routledge and Kegan Paul, 1959, (on Bentham, Fourier, Buckingham).

Toynbee, Arnold, *Cities of Destiny,* New York, McGraw-Hill, 1967.

Zehner, Robert B., "Neighborhood and Community Satisfaction in New Towns," *J. Amer. Inst. of Planners,* November 1971, 379–385.

1 Introduction

Bacon, Edmund, N., *Design of Cities,* New York, Viking Press, rev. ed., 1973.

Colin Clark, *Population Growth and Land Use,* New York, St. Martin, 1967.

Fourastié, Jean, *La Grande metamorphose du XXe siècle,* Paris, Presses Universitaires de France, 1961.

2 New capitals

Australian National Development Corporation, *16th Annual Report,* 1972–73.

Argan, Giulio, *The Renaissance City,* New York, George Braziller, 1969.

Bishop, Carl Whiting, "Ch'Ang-an: An Ancient Chinese Capital," in *Annual Reports of The Smithsonian Institution,* 1930, p. 570.

Chung, Hyung C., "Capital Cities of China," unpublished essay, Columbia University, 1968.

Costa, Lucio, *Plano-Piloto Para a Urbanizacao, Barra da Tiiuca a Jacarepagua,* Estado de Guanabara, 1969.

Creswell, K. A. C., *Early Muslim Architecture,* Baltimore, Penguin Books, 1958. (Chapter 8 on Round City of Al Mansur in Baghdad, 762 A.D.).

Doxiades Associates, "Islamabad—the Scale of the City and its Central Area," *Ekistics,* XIV, No. 83, 1962.

———, *Islamabad—Summary of Final Programme and Plan,* Athens, 1962.

———, "Islamabad: The Creation of a New Capital," in *Town Planning Review,* XXXVI, No. 1, 1965.

Egli, Ernst, *Geschichte des Stadtebaues,* 3 vols., Zurich-Erlenbach, E. Rentsch, 1959–67.

Epstein, David G., *Brasilia: Plan and Reality,* Berkeley, University of California Press, 1973.

Evenson, Norma, *Chandigarh,* Berkeley, University of California, 1966.

———, *Two Brazilian Capitals: Architecture & Urbanism in Rio de Janeiro and Brasilia,* New Haven, Yale University Press, 1973, chapter 9.

Hardoy, Jorge E., "The Planning of New Capital Cities," in *UNO Planning of Metropolitan Areas and New Towns,* New York, 1967, pp. 232–249.

———, "La Plata, Argentina's Nineteenth-Century New Town," Ibid., pp. 174–177.

———, *Urban Planning in Pre-Columbian America,* New York, George Braziller, 1968.

Haskell, Douglas, "Brasilia: A New Type of National City," *Architectural Forum,* November, 1970.

Hiraoka, Takeo and Imai, Kyochi, *Chuangan and Lo-yang,* Jinbunka Gaku Kendyusho, Kyoto, Kyoto University.

Holford, William, "The Future of Canberra," *The Town Planning Review,* XXIX, No. 3, 1958.

Hussey, Christopher, *The Life of Sir Edwin Lutyens,* London, Country Life, 1950.

Instituto Brasileiro de Estadistica, *Brasilia, 1970.*

Kite, Elisabeth S., *L'Enfant and Washington: 1791–92,* Baltimore, 1929.

Plan regulador conjunto de los partidos de Enseñada y La Plata, Buenos Aires, URBIS, 1961.

Le Corbusier, *Oeuvres Complètes,* 7 vols. (1910–1965), Zurich, Editions Artémis.

Lampl, Paul, *Cities and Planning in the Ancient Near East,* New York, George Braziller, 1968.

Lockhart, Laurence, "Shah Abbas's Isfahan," in Toynbee, *Cities of Destiny,* New York, McGraw-Hill, 1967, pp. 219–225.

McQuade, Walter, "Brasilia's Beginning," *Architectural Forum,* April, 1959.

The National Capital Development Corporation, *Tomorrow's Canberra,* Canberra, Australian National University Press, 1970.

Snyder, David A., "Alternative Perspectives on Brasilia, *Economic Geography.*

Talbot Rice, "Tamara: Eighteenth Century St. Petersburg," in Toynbee, *Cities of Destiny,* New York, McGraw-Hill, 1967, pp. 242–258.

National Capital Planning Commission; *A Plan for the Year 2000,* Washington, D.C., National Capital Regional Planning Council, June 1961.

Trewartha, Glenn T., "Chinese Cities: Origins and Functions," *Annals of the Association of American Geographers,* XIII, 1952.

Reps, John W, *Monumental Washington,* Princeton University Press, 1967.

Von Moos, Stanislas, "Chandigarh ville morte?" *Architecture d'Aujourd'hui,* No. 146, Oct.–Nov. 1969.

Ward-Perkins, J. B., *Cities of Ancient Greece and Italy: Planning in Antiquity,* New York, George Braziller, 1974.

Wilhelm, Jorge, *Brasilia 1960—Uma Interpretacao,* Acropole, Brasilia, 2nd ed., 1960.

Wright, Arthur F., "Changan," in Toynbee, *Cities of Destiny,* New York, McGraw-Hill, 1967, pp. 138–150.

3 Colonial towns   *Architetti Militari; Italiani nella Spagna nel Portogallo e nelle Colonia,* Genio Italiano, Seria quarta, III, 1937.

Beresford, Maurice, *New Towns of the Middle Ages, Town Plantation in England, Wales and Gascony,* New York, Praeger, 1967.

Boethius, Axel, "The Hellenized Italian Town," in *The Golden House of Nero,* Ann Arbor, University of Michigan, 1960.

Bridenbaugh, Carl, *Cities in the Wilderness,* 1625–1742, New York, The Ronald Press, 1938.

Burke, G. L., *The Making of Dutch Towns, 1956.* (Chap. III). Cleaver Hume Press, Ltd., London.

Camblin, Gilbert, *The Town in Ulster,* Belfast, 1951.

Chueca Goitia, Fernando y Torres Balbas, Leopoldo *Planos de ciudades iberoamericanas y filipinas,* Madrid, Instituto de Estudios de Administración local, 1951.

De la Croix, Horst, *Military Considerations in City Planning: Fortifications,* New York, George Braziller, 1972.

Davelaar, P., and Van Willigen, H., "Almere een nieuwe stad met een nieuwe conceptie," Stedebouw & Volkshuisvesting, 1971.

De Azevedo, Aroldo, "Vilas e cidades do Brasil, colonial," Sao Paolo, *Univ. de S.P. Boletim,* No. 208, 1956.

Dickinson, R. E., "The Development and Distribution of the Medieval German Town," *Geography,* XXVII, 1942.

Ebert, W., *Geschichte der Ostdeutschen Kolonisation,* Leipzig, 1967.

Eimer, Gerhard, *Die Stadtplanung im Schwedischen Ostseereich, 1600–1715,* Stockholm, Svenska Bokforlaget, 1961.

Floyd, T. B., *Town Planning in South Africa,* 1960.

Harris, Walter D., *The Growth of Latin American Cities,* Athens, Ohio, Ohio University Press, 1971.

Hofer, Paul, "Die Stadtgründungen des Mittelalters zwischen Genfersee und Rhein," in Boesch-Hofer, *Flugbild der Schweizerstadt,* Bern, Kummerly & Frey, 1963.

Lampl, op. cit.

Malisz, B., *Physical Planning for the Development of Satellite and New Towns,* Warsaw, paper submitted at the U.N. symposium on new towns, Moscow, 1964.

Martinez, Carlos, *Urbanismo en el Nuevo Reino de Granada,* Bogotá, Banco de la República, 1967.

Palm, Erwin Walter, "Los origenes del urbanismo municipal en America," in *Contribuciones a la historia municipal de America,* Mexico, Instituto Panamericano de Geografia y Historia, 1951.

Pinchas Geiger, Pedro, *Evoluçao da rêde urbana brasileira,* Instituo Nacional de Estudios Pedagogicos, Rio de Janeiro, 1963, pp. 424–434.

Pirenne, Henri, *Medieval Cities, Their Origins and the Revival of Trade,* Princeton University Press, 1925: New York, 1956.

Recopilación de Leyes de los Reynos de las Indias, facsimile reedition of the 4th printing of 1791, Madrid, 1943.

Reps, John W., *The Making of Urban America,* Princeton University Press, 1965.

Ricard, Robert, "La Plaza Mayor en Espagne et en Amérique Espagnole," in *Annales: Economies-Societés-Civilisations,* II, 4 (October–December, 1947), pp. 433–438.

Saalman, H., *Medieval Cities,* New York, George Braziller, 1968.

Shachar, Arie S., "Israel's Development Towns," *J. Amer. Inst. of Planners,* November, 1971.

Spiegel, Erika, *New Towns in Israel,* Stuttgart, Karl Kramer Verlag, 1966.

Stevin, Simon, *Materiae politicae Burgherlicke Stoffen,* Leiden, 1660, orig. 1590.

Torres-Balbas, L. et al., *Resúmen histórico del urbanismo en España,* Madrid, Instituto de Estudios de Administración Local, 1954.

Van Eesteren, C., *Stedebouwkundigplan voor Lelystad,* Gravenhage, Staatsuitgeverij, 1964.

Van der Wall, V. I., *Oude Hollandsche Bouwkunst in Indonesie,* Batavia, 1942.

Ward-Perkins, J. B., op. cit.

4 Industrial towns   *Ariashahr City Master Plan, GIPROGOR,* Moscow, U.S.S.R., State
Town Planning Institute, Feb., 1969.

Baranov, N. V., *Building New Towns,* Background Paper No.
11. for the U.N. Symposium on Moscow, 1964.

Buder, Stanley, "The Model Town of Pullman," *J. Amer. Inst.
or Planners,* Jan., 1967, pp. 2–10.

Choay, Françoise, *The Modern City: Planning in the 19th Century,* New York, George Braziller, 1969.

Collins, George, "Linear Planning Throughout the World," *J.
Soc. of Archit. Historians,* XVIII, Oct, 1959, pp. 74–93.

Corporación Venezolana de Guayana, *10 Años 1960–1970,*
Caracas, 1970.

Creese, Walter L., *The Search for Environment, The Garden
City: Before and After,* New Haven, Yale University Press,
1966.

CVG, *Informe Annual, 1965 La Ciudad,* separada, 1967, 1974,
CVG-EDELCA.

Epitèsi es Varosfejlesztesi Minisztèrium, *Orszàgos Települes-
fejlesztesi Konceptiò,* Budapest, 1971.

Evenson, Norma, *Le Corbusier: The Machine and the Grand
Design,* New York, George Braziller, 1969.

Galantay, E., Perez-Canto, J., and Weber, H., "Evaluation of
Sites for Focal Structures," CVG Staff Paper No. E-79,
August, 1963.

Garnier, Tony, *Une cité industrielle,* Paris, Vincent, 1918; 2 vols.,
second ed., Paris, Massin, 1929.

Grabania, M. *Nowe Tychy, miasto satelita,* Katowice, Slasky
Instytut, 1966.

Koenigsberger, Otto M., "New Towns in India," in *Town Planning Review,* July, 1962, 94–131.

Kosmin, Michel, *Ville Linéaire, Aménagement, Architecture,*
Paris, Vincent Fréal, 1952.

Llewelyn-Davies-Weeks-Forestier-Walker & Bor, *Development
Proposals for a New City at El Tablazo,* Caracas, February,
1969.

Mackenzie, Norman, "Elizabeth, an Australian New Town," in
Town and Country Planning, London, XXVIII, Nos. 8, 9,
Aug.–Sept., 1960, pp. 283–289.

Merlin, Pierre, *Nouvelle Planification et Urbanisme en Pologne,*
Paris, Cahiers I.A.U.R.P., XX, 1970.

Meibeyer, Wolfgang, "Monographie der Stadt Wolfsburg," in
Mittelstadt, Jancke-Verlag, Braunschweig, 1972.

Parkins, Maurice F., *City Planning in Soviet Russia,* Chicago,
University of Chicago Press, 1946.

Pawlowski, Christophe, *Tony Garnier,* Paris, Centre de Recherche d'Urbanisme, 1967.

Richardson, N. H., "A Tale of Two Cities in North West Canada," from *Plan Canada,* IV, no. 3, 1963, 111–125.

Robinson, I. M., *New Industrial Towns on Canada's Resource
Frontier,* University of Chicago, 1962.

Rodwin, Lloyd, *Planning Urban Growth and Regional Development: The Experience of the Guayana Program,* Cambridge,
Mass., M.I.T. Press, 1969.

Shkavirov V., et al, "The Building of New Towns in the USSR,"
Ekistics, November, 1964, 307–320.

Shkavirov V., et Smolar, I., "Planning of New Towns," *Arkhitektura SSSR,* 1966, No. 7.

Teut, Anna, *Architektur im dritten Reich,* Ulstein Bauwelt Fun-
damente, Berlin, 1967 (chapters XII & XIII).

Turner, Alan and Smulian, Jonathan, "New Cities in Venezuela," in *Town Planning Review*, XLII, No. 1, January, 1971, pp. 3–27. (For El Tablazo and El Tuy).

Union de Arquitectos Socialistas (Mexico) *Proyecto de la Ciudad Obrera en Mexico D.F.,* Cd. Sahagun., XVI Congreso International de Planificación, 1938.

Wiebenson, Dora, *Tony Garnier: The Cité Industrielle,* New York, George Braziller, 1969.

5 Decongestion

Aastrom Kell, *City Planning in Sweden,* Stockholm, The Swedish Institute, 1967.

Abercrombie, P., *Greater London, 1944,* London, HMSO, 1955.

Ahlberg, K. F., *Shopping Centers and Satellite Towns in the Stockholm Region,* background paper Conference on Regional Planning, Zurich, 1965.

Ashworth, William, *The Genesis of British Town Planning,* London, Routledge and Kegan Paul, 1954.

Bailey, James, ed., *New Towns in America: the Design and Development Process,* compiled by the American Institute of Architects.

Blake, Peter, "Walt Disney World," *Architectural Forum,* June, 1972, 24–41.

Bor, Walter, *The Making of Cities,* London, Leonard Hill, 1972 (appendix 24 on Milton Keynes; appendix 25 on Amherst, N.Y.).

Brooks, Richard, "Social Planning in Columbia," *J. Amer. Inst. of Planners,* November, 1971, 373–379.

Browne, Kenneth, "Test Case: Irvine New Town," *Architectural Review,* October, 1973.

Esquema Director Año 2000, Buenos Aires, Consejo Nacional del desarrollo, December, 1969.

Bunin, Andrei Vladimirovich, et al., *Gradostroitel'stvo,* Moscow: Akademiia Arkhitektury SSSR 1945.

Candilis-Josic-Woods, *Une décennie d'architecture et d'urbanisme,* Paris, Ed. Eyrolles, 1968 (Toulouse le Mirail and various urban design competitions).

Carruth, Eleanor, "The Big Move to New Towns," in *Fortune,* September 1971, 95–100.

Choay, op. cit.

Colin, Armand, *L'experience française des villes nouvelles,* Paris, 1970 (Vaudreuil, etc.).

Collins, George R, "The Ciudad Lineal of Madrid," in *J. Society of Arch. Historians,* XVIII, May 1959, 38–53.

Columbia (Maryland) Community Research and Development Corporation, *General Development Plan,* January, 1966.

Cumbernauld Development Corporation, *Cumbernauld New Town Preliminary Planning Proposals:* 1958, 1962, 1963; *Planning Proposals:* first revision, 1959; *Planning Proposals:* second revision, 1962; *Economic Assessment of Main Roads,* 1961, Feb. 1964.

Downs, Anthony, "Alternative Forms of Future Urban Growth in the USA," in *J. Amer. Inst. of Planners,* Jan. 1970.

Duquesne, Jean, *Vivre à Sarcelles?,* Paris, Editions Cujas, 1966.

"Evry: Centre urbain nouveau et ville nouvelle," Paris, *Cahiers I.A.U.R.P.,* vol. XV, May 1969.

"Evry I Concours d'aménagement urbain," *Cahiers I.A.U.R.P.,* XXXI, Paris, 1973.

Galantay, E. Y. "Black New Towns," in *Progressive Architecture,* August 1968, 126–137.

———, "Designing the Environment (Osaka)" in *The Nation,* Aug. 31. 1970, pp. 134–138.

Gibberd, Frederick, "New Towns of Britain," *J. Amer. Inst. of Architects,* March 1961.

Great Britain: New Towns Committee (Lord Reith, Chairman) *Final Report of the New Towns Committee,* Cmd. 6876, London, 1946.

Guertin, Pierre, "La ville nouvelle de Cumbernauld," *Urbanisme No. 106,* 1968.

Hall, Peter, *London 2000,* New York, Praeger.

———, *The World Cities,* New York, McGraw-Hill, 1966.

Harlow Development Corporation: *New Towns Population Survey 1964,* London Economic Intelligence Unit, 1965.

The Planning of a New Town (Hook), Greater London Council 1965.

Hilberseimer, Ludwig, *The New City: Principles of Planning,* Chicago, Theobald, 1944.

Hoppenfeld Morton, *The Columbia Process,* Letchworth, Garden City Press, Ltd., 1970.

Howard, Ebenezer, *Garden Cities of Tomorrow,* London, Faber and Faber, 1946. Originally published 1898, 1902.

The Irvine Company Annual Report, Newport Beach, California, 1973.

Irvine Development Corporation, *Irvine New Town,* 1971.

Isaacs, Reginald R., "The Neighborhood Theory," *J. Amer. Inst. of Planners,* XIV, Spring 1948, 15–23.

Jellicoe, G. A., *Motopia,* New York, Praeger, 1961.

Knyaziev, K. F., "Satellite Towns and the Development of Large Cities," published in *Izvestiia Akademiia Stroiteltsva Architektury,* 1960.

Laland, André et al, "Ville nouvelle d'Evry," in *Techniques et Architecture,* no. 5/ 32.

Llewelyn-Davies Weeks, et al, *Washington New Town,* December, 1966.

Mayer, Albert, *Greenbelt Towns Revisited,* Washington, D.C., H.U.D., 1968.

McFayden, Dugald, *Sir Ebenezer Howard and the Town Planning Movement,* Cambridge, Mass., MIT Press, 1971.

Merlin, Pierre, et al., *Villes nouvelles en Scandinavie,* IX, Paris, Institut d'Aménagement et d'Urbanisme de la Région Parisienne, 1967.

"Milton Keynes: A Progress Report," *Architectural Design,* June 1973.

"Milton Keynes," *Domus,* April 1973, 6–18.

Plan for Milton Keynes, vols. I and II, March 1970, The Milton Keynes Development Plan, M. Keynes Development Corporation, 1970.

Montgomery Village, Development proposal by Rogers, Taliaferro, Kostritsky & Lamb, Baltimore, 1964.

The Maryland National Capital Park and Planning Commission, *Master Plan for Germantown: A Corridor City,* Oct. 1966.

New Communities for New York, a report prepared by the New York State Urban Development Corporation, Albany, 1970.

The New Towns of Britain, Central Office of Information, Jan. 1972.

New York State Urban Development Acts of 1968, Urban Development Corporation, Albany, 1968.

Osborn, Frederick J., "Sir Ebenezer Howard: The Evolution of his Ideas," *Town Planning Review*, 21 Oct. 1950, p. 27.

————, and Whittick, Arnold, *The New Towns: The Answer to Megalopolis*, New York, McGraw-Hill, 1963.

Orangewood, Florida, Development Concept, Hart-Krivatsy-Stubee, Nov. 1970.

Perry, Clarence, "The Neighborhood Unit," in *Regional Plan of New York and its Environs*, VII, 1929.

"Reston Va.," *Architectural Design*, Feb. 1973.

Reston Quarterly Fact Sheet, Gulf Reston Co., Winter 1973, figures compiled as of January 1, 1973.

Reston Master Plan, Fairfax County, Virginia.

Rodwin, Lloyd, *The British New Towns Policy*, Cambridge, Harvard University Press, 1956.

Rodwin, Lloyd and Suskind, Lawrence, "New Communities and Urban Growth Strategies," *Congressional Record U.S. Senate*, 21 July 1972.

Runcorn Development Corporation, *Runcorn New Town*, Runcorn, England, 1967.

Senri New Town, Senboku New Town, Public Enterprise Bureau, Osaka Prefecture, 1970.

Stein, Clarence, *Toward New Towns for America*, Revised edition N.Y., Reinhold, 1957.

Stockholm: Urban Environment, Vällingby Fársta, Stockholms Stadsbygnadskontor, 1972.

"Thamesmead," *Architectural Forum*, July/August 1969.

Town and Country Planning Act, London, HMSO, 1968.

Tyrwhitt, Jacqueline, "The Size and Spacing of Urban Communities," *J. Amer. Inst. of Planners*, XV, Summer 1949, 10–17.

Ungers, O. M. and Ungers, Liselotte, "Nordwestzentrum" in *Architectural Forum*, Oct. 1970, 30–37.

Unwin, Sir Raymond, *Nothing Gained by Overcrowding*, London, Garden Cities and Town Planning Association, 1912.

————, *Town Planning in Practice*, London, Unwin, 1909.

"Villes nouvelles en Grande Bretagne," Paris, *Cahiers de I.A.U.R.P.*, XXI, 1970.

"La ville nouvelle de la Vallée de la Marne," Paris, *Cahiers I.A.U.R.P.*, XXI, 1970.

Ville nouvelle de la Vallée de la Marne, Noisiel, Mission d'Amemagement, 1970.

Von Hertzen, Heikki and Speiregen, Paul, *Tapiola, Building a New Town*, Cambridge Mass., MIT Press, 1971.

Wright, Frank Lloyd, *Broadacre City*, Taliesin Fellowship Publication, Oct. 1940, No. 1; G. R. Collins, "Broadacre City: Wright's Utopia Re-Considered," in *Four Great Makers of Modern Architecture*, New York, Columbia School of Architecture, 1963, pp. 58–75.

Yokkaichi City: Study of Land Use Planning. Government of Japan, Ministry of Construction Building Research Institute, Occasional Report No. 4, January 1961.

INDEX

Boldfaced numbers refer to plates. References to notes (n.) are given by chapter (Roman numeral) and number (Arabic numeral).

SOURCES OF ILLUSTRATIONS

Illustrations not credited below are in anonymous collections. All numbers refer to plate numbers, unless otherwise indicated.

Aerofilms, London: 82–85, 88, 89, 93

American Institute of Architects Journal: 90

Archivo de las Indias, Sevilla: 42–44, 46

G. C. Argan, *The Renaissance City,* New York, 1969: 9

Arkitektur SSSR, No. 7, 1966, "Planning of New Towns," by V. Shkvarikov and I. Smolar: 60

Asuntosaatio, Tapiola, Courtesy of: 107–109

Australian National Capital Development Corporation: 15–18

Bauwelt, No. 43/44, 1968: 65b

Budapest Technical University, Urban Design Department: 61, 62

A. W. Bunin, *Geschichte des Russischen Stadtebaues,* Berlin, 1961: 12a, b, c, fig. 6

Cahiers de l'Institut d'amenagement et d'Urbanisme de la région parisienne: "Evry," Vol. 15, May 1969: 113; "Concours Evry 1," Vol. 31, April 1973: 118

F. Choay, *The Modern City: Planning in the 19th Century,* New York, 1969: 41, 57

Erik Claeson, Stockholm: 105, 106

Le Corbusier, *Oeuvres completes:* 25, 26

Corporación Venezolana de Guayana, Courtesy of: 66, 67, 69, 70–72

Lucio Costa, Sao Paolo, Courtesy of: 76, fig. 3

K. A. C. Creswell, *A Short Account of Early Muslim Architecture,* Baltimore, 1958: 2

C. Doxiades, *Ekistics,* London, 1968: 27, 28

Egli, *Geschichte des Statdbaues,* III, Erlenbach-Zurich, 1967: 7, 36

Ekistics Magazine, Athens, Vol. 18, No. 108, Nov. 1964: 29, 30

Richard T. Ely, "Pullman: a Social Study," *Harper's Magazine,* Vol. 70, No. 417, 1885: 58

Etablissement Public d'Amenagement de la ville nouvelle de Cergy-Pontoise: 114, 115, 117

E. Y. Galantay: 19, 22 a & b, Figs. 1, 9

Geographic Institute, Wagner & Debes, Leipzig, 1910: 1

E. Gloeden, *Die Inflation der Gross-Stadte und ihre Heilungs-moglichkeiten,* Berlin, 1923: 80

Graduate School of Design, Harvard University: 129

Greater London Council: 86, 91, 92

Peter Hall, *The World Cities,* New York, 1966: 112

H. Heidersberger, Wolfsburg: 65, 65c

Her Majesty's Stationery Office, Crown copyright: 87

E. Howard, *Garden Cities of Tomorrow,* London, 1902: fig. 14

Instituto Brasileira do Geografia: 21

International Congress for Housing and Town Planning, Source XXIII, United Nations, 1956: fig. 10

Irvine Company/Irvine Development Corporation: 100, 101, 124, 125

Albert Jewett G. I. Official Records: 59

Clemens de Jonghe, Amsterdam, 1660: 39

P. Lampl, *Cities and Planning in the Ancient Near East,* New York, 1968: 33, 55

Lausanne, Swiss Federal Institute of Technology: 14, 35, 48, 51, 53

Library of Congress: 45, 49, 50

Milton Keynes Development Corporation, Courtesy of Derek Walker: 47, 74, 75a&b, 102, 103, fig. 13

Ministerio de Obras Públicas, Caracas, Llewelyn-Davies et al.: 73

Moscow, Strolizdat, 1962: fig. 11

New York State Development Corporation: 126

National Capital Development Land Agency, "Year 2000" Plan: 119

NOVACAP, Brasilia, Courtesy of: 23

Osaka, Public Enterprise Bureau, Courtesy of: 110, 111

F. J. Osborne & A. Whittick, *The New Towns,* New York, 1963: fig. 16

Waclaw Ostrowski, *L'Urbanisme contemporrain,* Centre de Recherche et d'urbanisme: figs. 7, 8

C. Y. Perry, *Regional Survey of New York and its Environs,* Vol. VII, New York, 1929: fig. 15

Préfecture de la Région Parisienne, Courtesy of: 116

Promotora Calitlan S. A., Courtesy of Prof. E. Escalante-E.: 77

C. B. Purdom, *The Building of Satellite Towns,* London 1949: 79

M. Ragon, *La Cité dans l'an 2000,* Paris: 128

Regional Plan Association, New York: 120

The Rouse Corporation, Columbia, Md., Courtesy of: 121–123

Runcorn Development Corporation, Courtesy of Arthur Ling: 96, 97, 99, fig. 17

Ryksdienst voor de Ijselmeerpolders, Ministerie von Verkeer en Waterstaat, The Hague, Courtesy of: 31, 32

Howard Saalman, *Medieval Cities,* New York, 1968: 37

Hideo Sasaki, Courtesy of: 127

Erika Spiegal, *New Towns in Israel,* 52, 54

Stadtplanungsamt, Wolfsburg: 63, 64

Stadtplanungsamt, Aero-Lux, Frankfurt/Main, Courtesy of: 65a

Stevenage Development Corporation, Courtesy of: 81

S. Stevin, *Materiae Politicae,* Leiden, 1660: 40

Henri Stierlin, *Iran of the Master Builders,* Geneva, 1971: 8

Stockholm Town Planning Office, Courtesy of: 104

Swissair Photo AG: 38

Urbanistica, no. 53: 94, 95, 98

J. B. Ward-Perkins, *Cities of Ancient Italy and Greece,* New York 1974: fig. 4

Herbert Wilhelmy, *Sudamerika im Spiegel seiner Staedte,* Hamburg, 1952: 20

Martin Zeiller, *Topographia Galliae,* 1656: 10

© 下出国雄 1969年 : 4, 5, fig. 2